DARK MODE EDITIONS

MEDITATIONS

DARK MODE EDITIONS: Meditations.

The authorised representative in the EEA is Simon and Schuster Netherlands BV, Herculesplein 96 3584 AA Utrecht, Netherlands.
(info@simonandschuster.nl)

Andrews McMeel Publishing
a division of Andrews McMeel Universal
1130 Walnut Street, Kansas City, Missouri 64106

www.andrewsmcmeel.com

6 27 28 29 30 SDB 10 9 8 7 6 5 4 3 2 1

ISBN: 979-8-8816-1035-7
Library of Congress Control Number: 2026930573

Edited by Monica Sweeney
Design by Joanna Williams
Illustrations used under license from Shutterstock

FSC
www.fsc.org
MIX
Paper | Supporting responsible forestry
FSC® C144853

DARK MODE EDITIONS

MEDITATIONS

Andrews McMeel
PUBLISHING®

TABLE OF CONTENTS

...

THE FIRST BOOK

1. I learned from my grandfather, Verus, to use good manners, and to put restraint on anger.

2. In the famous memory of my father I had a pattern of modesty and manliness.

3. Of my mother I learned to be pious and generous; to keep myself not only from evil deeds, but even from evil thoughts; and to live with a simplicity which is far from customary among the rich.

4. I owe it to my great-grandfather that I did not attend public lectures and discussions, but had good and able teachers at home; and I owe him also the knowledge that for things of this nature a man should count no expense too great.

5. My tutor taught me not to favor either green or blue at the chariot races, nor, in the contests of gladiators, to be a supporter either of light or heavy armed. He taught me also to endure labor; not to need many things; to serve myself without troubling others; not to intermeddle in the affairs of others, and not easily to listen to slanders against them.

6. Of Diognetus I had the lesson not to busy myself about vain things; not to credit the great professions of such as pretend to work wonders, or of sorcerers about their charms, and their expelling of Demons and the like; not to keep quails (for fighting or divination), nor to run after such things; to suffer freedom of speech in others, and to apply myself heartily to philosophy. Him also I must thank for my

hearing first Bacchius, then Tandasis and Marcianus; that I wrote dialogues in my youth, and took a liking to the philosopher's pallet and skins, and to the other things which, by the Grecian discipline, belong to that profession.

---

7. To Rusticus I owe my first apprehensions that my nature needed reform and cure; and that I did not fall into the ambition of the common Sophists, either by composing speculative writings or by declaiming harangues of exhortation in public; further, that I never strove to be admired by ostentation of great patience in an ascetic life, or by display of activity and application; that I gave over the study of rhetoric, poetry, and the graces of language; and that I did not pace my house in my senatorial robes, or practice any similar affectation. I observed also the simplicity of style in his letters, particularly in that which he wrote to my mother from Sinuessa. I learned from him to be easily appeased, and to be readily reconciled with those who had displeased me or given cause of offence, so soon as they inclined to make their peace; to read with care; not to rest satisfied with a slight and superficial

knowledge; nor quickly to assent to great talkers. I have him to thank that I met with the discourses of Epictetus, which he furnished me from his own library.

---

8. From Apollonius I learned true liberty, and tenacity of purpose; to regard nothing else, even in the smallest degree, but reason always; and always to remain unaltered in the agonies of pain, in the losses of children, or in long diseases. He afforded me a living example of how the same man can, upon occasion, be most yielding and most inflexible. He was patient in exposition; and, as might well be seen, esteemed his fine skill and ability in teaching others the principles of philosophy as the least of his endowments. It was from him that I learned how to receive from friends what are thought favors without seeming humbled by the giver or insensible to the gift.

---

9. Sextus was my pattern of a benign temper, and his family the model of a household governed by true paternal affection, and a steadfast purpose of living according to nature. Here I

could learn to be grave without affectation, to observe sagaciously the several dispositions and inclinations of my friends, to tolerate the ignorant and those who follow current opinions without examination. His conversation showed how a man may accommodate himself to all men and to all companies; for though companionship with him was sweeter and more pleasing than any sort of flattery, yet he was at the same time highly respected and reverenced. No man was ever happier than he in comprehending, finding out, and arranging in exact order the great maxims necessary for the conduct of life. His example taught me to suppress even the least appearance of anger or any other passion; but still, with all this perfect tranquility, to possess the tenderest and most affectionate heart; to be apt to approve others yet without noise; to have much learning and little ostentation.

---

10. I learned from Alexander the Grammarian to avoid censuring others, to refrain from flouting them for a barbarism, solecism, or any false pronunciation. Rather was I dexterously to pronounce the words rightly in my answer, confining approval or objection to the matter

itself, and avoiding discussion of the expression, or to use some other form of courteous suggestion.

---

11. Fronto made me sensible how much of envy, deceit and hypocrisy surrounds princes; and that generally those whom we account nobly born have somehow less natural affection.

---

12. I learned from Alexander the Platonist not often nor without great necessity to say, or write to any man in a letter, that I am not at leisure; nor thus, under pretext of urgent affairs, to make a practice of excusing myself from the duties which, according to our various ties, we owe to those with whom we live.

---

13. Of Catulus I learned not to condemn any friend's expostulation even though it were unjust, but to try to recall him to his former disposition; to stint no praise in speaking of my masters, as is recounted of Domitius and Athenodorus; and to love my children with true affection.

14. Of Severus, my brother, I learned to love my kinsmen, to love truth, to love justice. Through him I came to know Thrasea, Helvidius, Cato, Dion, and Brutus. He gave me my first conception of a Commonwealth founded upon equitable laws and administered with equality of right; and of a Monarchy whose chief concern is the freedom of its subjects. Of him I learned likewise a constant and harmonious devotion to Philosophy; to be ready to do good, to be generous with all my heart. He taught me to be of good hope and trustful of the affection of my friends. I observed in him candor in declaring what he condemned in the conduct of others; and so frank and open was his behavior, that his friends might easily see without the trouble of conjecture what he liked or disliked.

15. The counsels of Maximus taught me to command myself, to judge clearly, to be of good courage in sickness and other misfortunes, to be moderate, gentle, yet serious in disposition, and to accomplish my appointed task without repining. All men believed that he spoke as he thought; and whatever he did, they knew it was done with good intent. I never found him surprised or astonished at anything. He was

never in a hurry, never shrank from his purpose, was never at a loss or dejected. He was no facile smiler, but neither was he passionate or suspicious. He was ready to do good, to forgive, and to speak the truth, and gave the impression of unperverted rectitude rather than of a reformed character. No man could ever think himself despised by Maximus, and no one ever ventured to think himself his superior. He had also a good gift of humor.

---

16. I learned from my father gentleness and undeviating constancy in judgments formed after due reflection; not to be puffed up with glory as men understand it; to be laborious and assiduous. He taught me to give ready hearing to any man who offered anything tending to the common good; to mete out impartial justice to every one; to apprehend rightly when severity and when clemency should be used; to abstain from all impure lusts; and to use humanity towards all men. Thus, he left his friends at liberty to sup with him or not, to go abroad with him or not, exactly as they inclined; and they found him still the same if some urgent business had prevented them from obeying his commands. I learned of him accuracy and patience in council,

for he never quitted an enquiry satisfied with first impressions. I observed his zeal to retain his friends without being fickle or over fond; his contentment in every condition; his cheerfulness; his forethought about very distant events; his unostentatious attention to the smallest details; his restraint of all popular applause and flattery. Ever watchful of the needs of the Empire, a careful steward of the public revenue, he was tolerant of the censure of others in affairs of that kind. He was neither a superstitious worshipper of the Gods, nor an ambitious pleaser of men, nor studious of popularity, but in all things sober and steadfast, well skilled in what was honorable, never affecting novelties. As to the things which make the ease of life, and which fortune can supply in such abundance, he used them without pride, and yet with all freedom: enjoyed them without affectation when they were present, and when absent he found no want of them. No man could call him sophist, buffoon, or pedant. He was a man of ripe experience, a full man, one who could not be flattered, and who could govern himself as well as others. I further observed that he honored all who were true philosophers, without upbraiding the rest, and without being led astray by any. His manners were easy, his conversation delightful, but not cloying. He took regular but moderate care of his body, neither as one over fond of life or of the adornment of his person, nor as one who despised these things. Thus, through his own care, he seldom needed any medicines, whether salves or potions. It was his special merit to yield without envy to any who had acquired any special faculty, as either eloquence, or learning in the Law, in ancient customs, or the like; and he aided such men strenuously, so that every one of them might be regarded and esteemed for his special excellence. He observed carefully the ancient customs of his forefathers, and preserved, without appearance of affectation, the ways of his native land. He was not fickle and capricious, and loved not change of place or employment. After his violent fits of headache, he would return fresh and vigorous to his wonted affairs. Of secrets he had few, and these seldom, and such only as concerned public matters. He displayed discretion and moderation in exhibiting shows for the entertainment of the people, in his public works, in largesse and the like; and in all those things he acted like one who regarded only what was right and becoming in the things themselves, and not the reputation that might follow after. He never bathed at unseasonable hours, had no vanity in building, was never solicitous either about his food or about the make or color of his clothes, or about the beauty of his servants. His dress came from Lorium—his villa on the coast—and was of Lanuvian wool for the most part. It is remembered how he used the tax-collector at Tusculum who asked his pardon, and all his behavior was of a piece with that. He was far from being inhuman, or implacable, or violent; never doing anything with such keenness that one could say he was sweating about it, in all things he reasoned distinctly, as one at leisure, calmly, regularly, resolutely, and consistently. A man might fairly apply that to him which is recorded of Socrates: that he could both abstain from and enjoy these things, in want whereof many show themselves weak, and, in the possession, intemperate. To be strong in abstinence and temperate in enjoyment, to be sober in both—these are qualities of a man of perfect and invincible soul, as was shown in the sickness of Maximus.

---

17. To the Gods, I owe it that I had good grandfathers and parents, a good sister, good teachers, good servants, good kinsmen, and friends, good almost all of them. I have to thank them that I never through haste and rashness offended any of them; though my temper was such as

might have led me to it had occasion offered. But by their goodness no such concurrence of circumstances happened as could discover my weakness. I am further thankful that I was not longer brought up with my grandfather's concubine, that I retained my modesty, and refrained even longer than need have been from the pleasures of love. To the Gods it is due that I lived under the government of such a prince and father as could take from me all vain glory, and convince me that it was not impossible for a prince to live in a court without guards, gorgeous robes, torches, statues, or such pieces of state and magnificence; but that he may reduce himself almost to the state of a private man, and yet not become more mean or remiss in those public affairs wherein power and authority are requisite. I thank the Gods that I have had such a brother as by his disposition might stir me to take care of myself, while at the same time he delighted me by his respect and love. I thank them that my children neither wanted good natural dispositions nor were deformed in body. I owe it to their good guidance that I made no greater progress in rhetoric and poetry, and in other studies which might have engrossed my mind had I found myself successful in them. By the Gods' grace I forestalled the wishes of those by whom I was brought up, in promoting them to the dignities they seemed most to desire; and I did not put them off with the hope that, since they were but young, I would do it hereafter. I owe to the Gods that I ever knew Apollonius, Rusticus and Maximus; that I have had occasion often and effectually to meditate with myself and enquire what is truly the life according to Nature. And, as far as lies within the dispensation of the Gods to give suggestion, help, or inspiration, there is nothing to prevent my having already realized that life. I have fallen short of it by my own fault, and because I gave no heed to the inward monitions and almost direct instructions of the Gods, to whom be thanks that my body hath so long endured the stress of such a life as I have led. By their goodness I never had to do with either Benedicta or Theodotus; and afterwards, when I fell into some foolish passions, I was soon cured. I give thanks that, having often been displeased with Rusticus, I never did anything to him which afterwards I might have had occasion to repent; that, though my mother was destined to die young, she lived with me all her later years; that, as often as I inclined to succor any who were either poor or had fallen into some distress, I was never answered that there was not ready money enough to do it, and that I myself never had need of the like succor from another.

I must be grateful, too, that I have such a wife, so obedient, so loving, so ingenuous; that I had choice of fit and able men to whom I might commit the education of my children. I have received divine aids in dreams; as in particular, how I might stay my spitting of blood and cure my vertigo; which good fortune happily fell to me at Caieta. The Gods watched over me also when I first applied myself to philosophy. For I fell not into the hands of any Sophist, nor sat poring over many volumes, nor devoted myself to solving syllogisms, or stargazing. That all these things should so happily fall out there was great need both for the help of fortune and for the aid of the Gods.

IN THE COUNTRY OF THE QUADI, BY THE GRANUA.

THE SECOND BOOK

1. Say this to yourself in the morning: Today I shall have to do with meddlers, with the ungrateful, with the insolent, with the crafty, with the envious and the selfish. All these vices have beset them, because they know not what is good and what is evil. But I have considered the nature of the good, and found it beautiful: I have beheld the nature of the bad, and found it ugly. I also understand the nature of the evildoer, and know that he is my brother, not because he shares with me the same blood or the same seed, but because he is a partaker of the same mind and of the same portion of immortality. I therefore cannot be hurt by any of these, since none of them can involve me in any baseness. I cannot be angry with my brother, or sever myself from him, for we are made by nature for mutual assistance, like the feet, the hands, the eyelids, the upper

and lower rows of teeth. It is against nature for men to oppose each other; and what else is anger and aversion?

---

2. All that I am is either flesh, breath, or the ruling part. Cast your books from you; distract yourself no more; for you have not the right to do so. Like one at the point of death despise this flesh, this corruptible bone and blood, this network texture of nerves, veins, and arteries. Consider, too, what breath is—mere air, and that always changing, expelled and inhaled again every moment. The third is the ruling part. As to this, take heed, now that you are old, that it remains no longer in servitude; that it be no more dragged hither and thither like a puppet by every selfish impulse. Repine no more at what fate now sends, nor dread what may befall you hereafter.

---

3. Whatever the Gods ordain is full of wise forethought. The workings of chance are not apart from nature, and not without connection and intertexture with the designs of Providence. Providence is the source of all things; and,

besides, there is necessity, and the utility of the Universe, of which you are a part. For, to every part of a being, that is good which springs from the nature of the whole and tends to its preservation. Now, the order of Nature is preserved in the changes of elements, just as it is in the changes of things that are compound. Let this suffice you, and be your creed unchangeable. Put from you the thirst of books, that you may not die murmuring, but meekly, and with true and heartfelt gratitude to the Gods.

---

4. Think of your long procrastination, and of the many opportunities given you by the Gods, but left unused. Surely it is high time to understand the Universe of which you are a part, and the Ruler of that Universe, of whom you are an emanation; that a limit is set to your days, which, if you use them not for your enlightenment, will depart, as you yourself will, and return no more.

5. Hourly and earnestly strive, as a Roman and a man, to do what falls to your hand with perfect unaffected dignity, with kindliness, freedom and justice, and free your soul from every other imagination. This you will accomplish if you perform each action as if it were your last, without willfulness, or any passionate aversion to what reason approves; without hypocrisy or selfishness, or discontent with the decrees of Providence. You see how few things it is necessary to master in order that a man may live a smooth-flowing, God-fearing life. For of him that holds to these principles the Gods require no more.

6. Go on, go on, O my soul, to affront and dishonor yourself! The time that remains to honor yourself will not be long. Short is the life of every man; and yours is almost spent; spent, not honoring yourself, but seeking your happiness in the souls of other men.

7. Cares from without distract you: take leisure, then, to add some good thing to your knowledge; have done with vacillation, and avoid the other error. For triflers, too, are they who, by their activities, weary themselves in life, and have no settled aim to which they may direct, once and for all, their every desire and project.

8. Seldom are any found unhappy from not observing what is in the minds of others. But such as observe not well the stirrings of their own souls must of necessity be unhappy.

9. Remember always what the nature of the Universe is, what your own nature is, and how these are related—the one to the other. Remember what part your qualities are of the qualities of the whole, and that no man can prevent you from speaking and acting always in accordance with that nature of which you

10. In comparing crimes together, as, according to the common idea, they may be compared, Theophrastus makes the true philosophical distinction, that those committed from motives of pleasure are more heinous than those which are due to passion. For he who is a prey to passion is clearly turned away from reason by some spasm and convulsion that takes him unawares. But he who sins from desire is conquered by pleasure, and so seems more incontinent and more effeminate in his vice. Justly then, and in a truly philosophical spirit, he says that sin, for pleasure's sake, is more wicked than sin which is due to pain. For the latter sinner was sinned against, and so driven to passion by his wrongs, while the former set out to sin of his own motion, and was led into ill-doing by his own lust.

---

11. Do every deed, speak every word, think every thought in the knowledge that you may end your days any moment. To depart from men, if there be really Gods, is nothing terrible. The Gods could bring no evil thing upon you. And if there be no Gods, or if they have no regard to human affairs, why should I desire to live in a world void of Gods and without Providence? But Gods

there are, and assuredly they regard human affairs; and they have put it wholly in man's power that he should not fall into what is truly evil. And of other things, had any been bad, they would have made provision also that man should have the power to avoid them altogether. For how can that make a man's life worse which does not corrupt the man himself? Presiding Nature could not in ignorance, or in knowledge impotent, have omitted to prevent or rectify these things. She could not fail us so completely that, either from want of power or want of skill, good and evil should happen promiscuously to good men and to bad alike. Now death and life, glory and reproach, pain and pleasure, riches and poverty—all these happen equally to the good and to the bad. But, as they are neither honorable nor shameful, they are therefore neither good nor evil.

---

12. It is the office of our rational power to apprehend how swiftly all things vanish; how the corporeal forms are swallowed up in the material world, and the memory of them in the tide of ages. Such are all the things of sense, especially those which ensnare us with pleasure or terrify us with pain, or those things which

vanity trumpets in our ears. How mean, how despicable, how sordid, how perishable, how dead are they! What are they whose opinions and whose voices bestow renown? What is it to die? Your mind can tell you that, did a man think of it alone, and, by close consideration, strip it of its ghastly trappings, he would no longer deem it anything but a work of Nature. To dread a work of Nature is a childish thing, and this is, indeed, not only Nature's work, but beneficial to her. Your reason tells you how man reaches God, and through what part, and what is the state of that part, when he has attained unto him.

---

13. Nothing, says the poet, is more miserable than to range over all things, to spy into the depths of the earth, and search, by conjecture, into the souls of those around us, yet not to perceive that it is enough for a man to devote himself to that divinity which is within him, and to pay it genuine worship. And this worship consists in keeping it pure from every passion and folly, and from repining at anything done by Gods or men. The work of the Gods is to be reverenced for its excellence. The works of men should be dear for the sake of the bond of kinship, or pitied, as we

must pity them sometimes, for their lack of the knowledge of good and evil. And men are not less maimed by this defect than by their want of power to know white from black.

---

14. Though you should live three thousand years or as many myriads, yet remember that no man loses any other life than that which now lives, nor lives any other than that which he is now losing. The longest and the shortest lives come to one effect. The present moment is the same for all men, and their loss, therefore, is equal, for it is clear that what they lose in death is but a fleeting instant of time. No man can lose either the past or the future, for how can a man be deprived of what he has not? These two things then are to be remembered: First, that all things recur in cycles, and are the same from everlasting, and that, therefore, it matters nothing whether a man shall contemplate these same things for one hundred years, or for two hundred, or for an infinite stretch of time: and, secondly, that he who lives longest and he who dies soonest have an equal loss in death. The present moment is all of which either is deprived, since that is all he has. No man can be robbed of that which he has not.

15. Beyond opinion there is nothing. The objections to this saying of Monimus the Cynic are obvious. But obvious also is the utility of what he said, if one accepts his pleasantry as far as truth will warrant it.

---

16. Man's soul dishonors itself, firstly and chiefly when it does all it can to become an excrescence, and as it were an abscess on the Universe. To fret against any particular event is to revolt against the general law of Nature, which comprehends the order of all events whatsoever. Again, it is dishonor for the soul when it has aversion to any man, and opposes him with intention to hurt him, as wrathful men do. Thirdly, it affronts itself when conquered by pleasure or pain; fourthly, when it does or says anything hypocritically, feignedly or falsely; fifthly, when it does not direct to some proper end all its desires and actions, but exerts them inconsiderately and without understanding. For even the smallest things should be referred to the end, and the end of rational beings is to follow the order and law of the venerable state and polity which comprehends them all.

17. The duration of man's life is but an instant; his substance is fleeting, his senses dull; the structure of his body corruptible; the soul but a vortex. We cannot reckon with fortune, or lay our account with fame. In fine, the life of the body is but a river, and the life of the soul a misty dream. Existence is a warfare, and a journey in a strange land; and the end of fame is to be forgotten. What then avails to guide us? One thing, and one alone—Philosophy. And this consists in keeping the divinity within inviolate and intact; victorious over pain and pleasure; free from temerity, free from falsehood, free from hypocrisy; independent of what others do or fail to do; submissive to hap and lot, which come from the same source as we; and, above all, with equanimity awaiting death, as nothing else than a resolution of the elements of which every being compounded. And, if in their successive interchanges no harm befalls the elements, why should one suspect any in the change and dissolution of the whole? It is natural, and nothing natural can be evil.

AT CARNUNTUM.

THE THIRD BOOK

1. Man must consider, not only that each day part of his life is spent, and that less and less remains to him, but also that, even if he lives longer, it is very uncertain whether his intelligence will suffice as heretofore for the understanding of his affairs, and for grasping that knowledge which aims at comprehending things human and divine. When dotage begins, breath, nourishment, fancy, impulse, and so forth will not fail him. But self-command, accurate appreciation of duty, power to scrutinize what strikes his senses, or even to decide whether he should take his departure, all powers, indeed, which demand a well-trained understanding, must be extinguished in him. Let him be up and doing then, not only because death comes nearer every day, but because understanding and intelligence often leave us before we die.

Observe what grace and charm appear even in the accidents that accompany Nature's work. Thus, some parts of a loaf crack and burst in the baking; and this cracking, though in a manner contrary to the design of the baker, looks well and invites the appetite. Figs, too, gape when at their ripest, and in ripe olives the very approach to rotting adds a special beauty to the fruit. The droop of ears of corn, the bent brows of the lion, the foam at a boar's mouth, and many other things, are far from comely in themselves, yet, since they accompany the works of Nature, they make part of her adornment, and rejoice the beholder. Thus, if a man be sensitive to such things, and have a more than common penetration into the constitution of the whole, scarce anything connected with Nature will fail to give him pleasure, as he comes to understand it. Such a man will contemplate in the real world the fierce jaws of wild beasts with no less delight than when sculptors or painters set forth for him their presentments. With like pleasure will his chaste eyes behold the maturity and grace of old age in man or woman, and the inviting charms of youth. Many such things will strike him, things not credible to the many, but which come to him alone who is truly familiar with the works of Nature and near to her own heart

3. Hippocrates, who had healed many diseases, himself fell sick, and died. The Chaldeans foretold the fatal hours of multitudes, and afterwards fate carried themselves away. Alexander, Pompey, and Gaius Caesar, who so often razed whole cities, and cut off in battle so many myriads of horses and feet, at last departed from this life themselves. Heraclitus, after his many speculations on the conflagration of the world, died, swollen with water and plastered with cow dung. Vermin destroyed Democritus; Socrates was killed by vermin of another sort. What of all this? You have gone aboard, made your voyage, come to harbor. Disembark: if into another life, there will God be also; if into nothingness, at least you will have done with bearing pain and pleasure, and with your slavery to this vessel so much meaner than its slave. For the soul is intelligence and deity, the body dust and corruption.

---

4. Waste not what remains of life in consideration about others, when it makes not for the common good. Be sure you are neglecting other work if you busy yourself with what such a one is doing and why, with what he is saying, thinking, or scheming. All such things do but divert you from the steadfast guardianship of your own soul. It

behooves you, then, in every train of thought to shun all that is aimless or useless, and, above all, everything officious or malignant. Accustom yourself so, and only so, to think, that, if any one were suddenly to ask you, "Of what are you thinking now?" you could answer frankly and at once, "Of so and so." Then it will plainly appear that you are all simplicity and kindliness, as befits a social being who takes little thought for enjoyment or any phantom pleasure; who spurns contentiousness, envy, or suspicion; or any passion the harboring of which one would blush to own. For such a man, who has finally determined to be henceforth among the best, is, as it were, a priest and minister of the Gods, using the spirit within him, which preserves a man unspotted from pleasure, unwounded by any pain, inaccessible to all insult, innocent of all evil; a champion in the noblest of all contests—the contest for victory over every passion. He is penetrated with justice; he welcomes with all his heart whatever befalls, or is appointed by Providence. He troubles not often, or ever without pressing public need, to consider what another may say, or do, or design. Solely intent upon his own conduct, ever mindful of his own concurrent part in the destiny of the Universe, he orders his conduct well, persuaded that his part is good. For the lot appointed to every man is part of the law of all things as well as a law for him. He forgets not that all rational beings are akin, and that the love of all mankind is part of the nature of man; also, that we must not think as all men think, but only as those who live a life accordant with nature. As for those who live otherwise, he remembers always how they act at home and abroad, by night and by day, and how and with whom they are found in company. And so, he cannot esteem the praise of such, for they enjoy not their own approbation.

---

5. In action be neither grudging, nor selfish, nor ill-advised, nor constrained. Let not your thoughts be adorned with overmuch nicety. Be not a babbler or a busybody. Let the God within direct you as a manly being, as an elder, a statesman, a Roman, and a ruler, standing prepared like one who awaits the recall from life, in marching order; requiring neither an oath nor the testimony of any man. And withal, be cheerful, and independent of the assistance and the peace that comes from others; for, it is a man's duty to stand upright, self-supporting, not supported.

If in the life of man you find anything better than justice, truth, sobriety, manliness; and, in sum, anything better than the satisfaction of your soul with itself in that wherein it is given to you to follow right reason; and with fate in that which is determined beyond your control; if, I say, you find aught better than this, then turn thereto with all your heart, and enjoy it as the best that is to be found. But if nothing seems to you better than the divinity seated within you, which has conquered all your impulses, which sifts all your thoughts, which, as Socrates said, has detached itself from the promptings of sense, and devoted itself to God and to the love of mankind; if you find every other thing small and worthless compared with this, see that you give place to no other which might turn, divert, or distract you from holding in highest esteem the good which is especially and properly your own. For it is not permitted to us to substitute for that which is good in reason or in fact anything not agreeable thereto, such as the praise of the many, power, riches, or the pursuit of pleasure. All these things may seem admissible for a moment; but presently they get the upper hand, and lead us astray. But do you, I say, frankly and freely choose the best, and keep to it. The best is what is for your advantage. If now you choose what is for your spiritual advantage, hold it fast; if what is for your bodily advantage, admit that it is so chosen, and keep your choice with all modesty. Only see that you make a sure discrimination.

---

7. Never esteem aught of advantage which will oblige you to break your faith, or to desert your honor; to hate, to suspect, or to execrate any man; to play a part; or to set your mind on anything that needs to be hidden by wall or curtain. He who to all things prefers the soul, the divinity within him, and the sacred cult of its virtues, makes no tragic groan or gesture. He needs neither solitude nor a crowd of spectators; and, best of all, he will live neither seeking nor shunning death. Whether the soul shall use its surrounding body for a longer or shorter space is to him indifferent. Were he to depart this moment, he would go as readily as he would do any other seemly and proper action, holding one thing only in lifelong avoidance—to find his soul in any case unbefitting an intelligent social being.

8. In the soul of the chastened and purified man you would find nothing putrid, foul, or festering. Fate does not cut off his life before its proper end; as one would say of an actor who left the stage before his part was ended, or he had reached his appointed exit. There remains nothing servile or affected, nothing too conventional or too seclusive, nothing that fears censure or courts concealment.

---

9. Hold in honor the faculty which forms opinions. It depends on this faculty alone that no opinion your soul entertains be inconsistent with the nature and constitution of the rational being. It ensures that we form no rash judgments, that we are kindly to men, and obedient to the Gods.

---

10. Cast from you then all other things, retaining these few. Remember also that every man lives only this present moment, which is a fleeting instant: the rest of time is either spent or quite unknown. Short is the time which each of us has to live, and small the corner of the earth he has to live in. Short is the longest posthumous fame,

and this preserved through a succession of poor mortals, soon themselves to die; men who knew not themselves, far less those who died long ago.

---

11. To these maxims, add this other: Accurately define or describe everything that strikes your imagination, so that you may see and distinguish what it is in naked essence, and what it is in its entirety; that you may tell yourself the proper name of the thing itself, and the names of the parts of which it is compounded, and into which it will be resolved. Nothing makes mind greater than the power to enquire into all things that present themselves in life; and, while you examine them, to consider at the same time of what fashion is the Universe, and what is the function in it of these things, of what importance they are to the whole, of what to man who is a citizen of that highest city of which all other cities are but households. Consider what is this thing that now makes an impression on you, of what it is composed, and how long it is destined to endure. Consider also for what virtue it calls; whether it be gentleness, courage, truthfulness, fidelity, simplicity, independence, or any other. Say, therefore, of each event: "This comes from

God," or "This comes from the conjunction and intertexture of the strands of fate, or from some chance or hazard of that kind," or "This comes from one of my own tribe, from my kinsman, from my friend. He is, indeed, ignorant of what accords with nature; but I am not, and will therefore use him kindly and justly, according to the natural and social law. As to things indifferent, I strive to appraise them at their proper value."

---

12. If you discharge your present duty with firm and zealous, yet kindly, observance of the laws of reason; if you regard no by-gains, but keep pure within you your immortal part, as if obliged to restore it at once to him who gave it; if you hold to this with no further desires or aversions, and be content with the natural discharge of your present task, and with the heroic sincerity of all you say or utter, you will live well. And herein no man can hinder you.

---

13. As surgeons have ever their knives and instruments at hand for the sudden emergencies of their art, so do you keep ready the principles requisite for understanding things divine and

human, and for doing all things, even the least important, in the remembrance of the bond between the two. For in neglecting this, you will scant your duty both to Gods and men.

14. Cease your wandering, for you are not like to read again your own memoirs, or the deeds of the ancient Greeks and Romans, or those collections from the writings of others that you laid up for your old age. Hasten then to your proper end. Fling away vain hopes, and, if you have any care for yourself, fly to your own succor while yet you may.

15. Men understand not all that is signified by the words—to steal, to sow, to buy, to rest, to see what is to be done. For it is not the bodily eye but another sort of sight that must discern these things.

16. We have body, soul, and intelligence. To the body belong the senses, to the soul the passions, to the intelligence principles. To be affected by

the imagery of sense belongs to the beasts of the field no less than to us. To be swayed by gusts of passion is common to us with the wild beasts, with the most effeminate wretches, with Nero and with Phalaris. Moreover, the possession of a mind to guide us to what seems fitting is shared by us, with atheists, with traitors to their country, and with such as shut their doors and sin. If, then, all the rest is common as we have seen, there remains to the good man this special excellence; to welcome with pleasure all that happens or is ordained, not to defile the divinity enthroned in his breast, not to perturb it with a crowd of images, but to preserve it in tranquility, and obey it as a God: to observe truth in all he says, and justice in his every action. And though others may not believe that he lives thus in simplicity, modesty, and contentment, he neither takes this unbelief amiss from any one, nor quits the road which leads to the true end of life, at which he ought to arrive pure, calm, ready to take his departure, and accommodated without compulsion to his fate.

THE FOURTH BOOK

1. The power which rules within us, when its state is accordant with nature, so acts in every occurrence as easily to adapt itself to all present or possible situations. It requires no set material to work upon, but, under proper reservation, needs but the incitement to pursue, and makes matter for its activities out of every opposition. Even so a fire masters that which is cast upon it, and though a small flame would have been extinguished, your great blaze quickly makes the added fuel its own, consumes it, and grows mightier therefrom.

2. Let no action be done at random, nor otherwise than in complete accordance with the principles involved.

---

3. Men seek retirement in the country, on the seacoast, in the mountains; and you too have frequent longings for such distractions. Yet surely this is great folly, since you may retire into yourself at any hour you please. Nowhere can a man find any retreat more quiet and more full of leisure than in his own soul; especially when there is that within it on which, if he but look, he is straightway quite at rest. And rest I hold to be naught else but perfect order in the soul. Constantly, therefore, allow yourself this retirement, and so renew yourself. Have also at hand thoughts brief and fundamental, which readily may occur; sufficing to shut out the discordant clamor of the world, and to send you back without fretting at the task to which you return. For at what do you fret? At the wickedness of mankind. Recollect the maxim that all reasoning beings are created for one another, that to bear with them is a part of justice, and that they cannot help their sin. Remember how many of those who lived in enmity, suspicion, and hatred, at daggers drawn, have been stretched on their

funeral pyres, and turned to ashes. Remember and cease from your complaints. Is it your allotted part in the world's destiny that chagrins you? Be calm, and renew your knowledge of the alternative, that "Either providence directs the world, or there is nothing but unguided atoms;" and recollect the many proofs that the Universe is as it were a state. Do the ills of the body still have power to touch you? Reflect that the mind, once withdrawn within itself, once grown conscious of its own power, has no concern with the motions, rough or smooth, of the breathing body. Remember, too, all that you have heard and assented to concerning pain and pleasure. Are you distracted by the poor thing called fame? Think how swiftly all things are forgotten. Behold the chaos of eternity which besets us on either side. Think how empty is the noisy echo of acclamation; how fickle and how scant of judgment are they who would seem to praise us, and how narrow the bounds within which their praise is confined. All the earth is but a point in the Universe; how small a corner of that little is inhabited, and even there how few are they and of how little worth who are to praise us! Remember then that there ever remains for you retirement into the little field within. And, above all, be neither distraught nor overstrained. Hold fast your freedom: consider all things as a man of courage, as a human being, as a citizen, as a mortal. Readiest among the principles to which you look let there be these two: Firstly, things external do not touch the soul, but remain powerless without; and all trouble comes from what we think of them within. Secondly, all things visible change in a moment, and are gone forever. Recollect all the changes of which you have yourself been a witness. The world is a succession of changes: life is but thought.

---

4. If mind be common to us all, the reason in virtue of which we are rational is also common; so too is the power which bids us do or not do. Therefore, we have all a common law; and if so, we are fellow citizens and members of some common polity. The Universe, then, must in a manner be a state, for of what other common polity can all mankind be said to be members? Wherefore it is from this common state that we derive our intellectual power, our reason, and our law; or whence do we derive them? For that which is earthy in me is derived from earth, my moisture from some other element, my breath and what is warm or fiery from their proper sources. And therefore, as nothing can arise from nothing or return thereto, my intellectual part has also a source.

5. Death, like birth, is a mystery of nature; the one a compounding of elements, the other a resolution into the same. In neither is there anything shameful or against the nature of the rational animal, or contrary to the law of its constitution.

---

6. It is fate that such actions should come from such men. He who would have it otherwise would have figs without juice. This, too, you should remember: that in a very short time both you and he must die; and a little after not even the name of either shall remain.

---

7. Suppress the thought; and the cry "I am hurt!" is gone. Suppress "I am hurt!" and you suppress the injury.

---

8. What makes not a man worse than he was, makes not his life worse, nor hurts him without or within.

9. The law of utility must act so.

---

10. All that happens, happens right: you will find it so if you observe narrowly. I mean not only according to a natural order, but according to our idea of justice, and, as it were, by the action of one who distributes according to merit. Go on then observing this as you have begun, and whatever you do, let your aim be goodness, goodness as it is rightly understood. Hold to this in every action.

---

11. Think not as your insulter judges or wishes you to judge, but see things as they truly are.

---

12. For two things be ever ready: First, to do that only which reason, the sovereign and legislative faculty, suggests for the good of mankind. Secondly, to change your course on meeting anyone who can correct and alter your opinion. But let the change be made because you really believe it to be in the interest of justice or the public good, or such like, and not with any view to pleasure or glory for yourself.

13. Have you reason? I have. Why then do you not use it? When it performs its proper office what more do you require?

---

14. You exist as part of a whole. You will disappear again in that which produced you; or rather you will change and be resumed again into the productive intelligence.

---

15. Many grains of frankincense are laid on the same altar. One falls soon, another later. It makes no difference.

---

16. Within ten days, if you return to the observance of moral principles and to the cult of reason, you will appear a God to them who now esteem you a wild beast or an ape.

---

17. Order not your life as though you had ten thousand years to live. Fate hangs over you. While you live, while yet you may, be good.

18. How much he gains in leisure who looks not to what his neighbors say, or do, or intend; but considers only how his own actions may be just and holy, looking not, as Agathon says, to the moral example of others, but running a straight course and never turning therefrom.

19. He who is careful and troubled about the fame which is to live after him considers not that each one of those who remember him must very soon die himself, and thereafter also the succeeding generation, until every memory of him, handed on by excited and ephemeral admirers, dies utterly away. Grant that your memory is immortal, and those immortal who retain it; yet what is that to you? I ask not, what is that to the dead? But to the living what is the profit in praise, except it be in some convenience that it brings? And you now abandon what nature has put in your power in order to set your hopes upon the report of others.

20. Whatever is beautiful at all is beautiful in itself. Its beauty ends there, and praise has no part in it. Nothing is the better or the worse for being

praised; and this holds also of what is beautiful in the common estimation: of material forms and works of art. Thus, true beauty needs nothing beyond itself, any more than law, or truth, or kindness, or honor. For none of these gets a single grace from praise or one blot from censure. Does the emerald lose its virtue if one praises it not? Can one by scanting praise depreciate gold, ivory, or purple, a lyre or a dagger, a flower or a shrub?

---

21. If our souls survive us, how, you ask, has the air contained them from eternity? How, I answer, does the earth contain so many bodies buried during so long a time? Just as corpses, after remaining for a while in the earth, change, and are dissipated to make room for others; so also the souls, liberated into air, remain for a little, and then are changed, diffused, rekindled, and resumed into the universal productive spirit; and so give way to others who come to take their places. This may serve for an answer, on the supposition that the soul survives the body. But we have not merely to consider the number of bodies thus buried in the earth. There are also all the living creatures eaten day by day by ourselves and other animals. How great a

multitude of them is thus consumed, and as it were buried in the bodies of those who feed upon them. Yet there is ever space to contain them, owing to the changes into blood, air, and fire. What, then, is the key to this enquiry? Discrimination of matter and cause.

---

22. Swerve not from your path. In every impulse render justice its due, and in all thinking be sure that you understand.

---

23. I am in tune with all that is of your harmony, O Nature. For me nothing is too early and nothing is too late that comes in your good time. All is fruit to me, O Nature, that your seasons bring. From you are all things, you comprehend all, and all returns to you. The poet says, "O dear City of Cecrops!" Shall I not say, "Dear City of God!"

---

24. "Do few things," says the philosopher, "if you would have quiet." This is perhaps a better saying, "Do what is necessary, do what the reason of the being that is social in its nature directs, and do it in

the spirit of that direction." By this you will attain the calm that comes from virtuous action, and that calm also which comes from having few things to do. Most things you say and do are not necessary. Have done with them, and you will be more at leisure and less perturbed. On every occasion, then, ask yourself the question, Is this thing not unnecessary? And put away not only unnecessary deeds but unnecessary thoughts, for by so doing you will avoid all superfluous actions.

---

25. Make trial how the life of a good man succeeds with you, the life of one who is content with the lot appointed him by Providence, and satisfied with the justice of his own actions and the benevolence of his disposition.

---

26. You have seen the other state, make trial also of this. Avoid perplexity; seek simplicity. Has a man sinned? He bears his own sin. Has aught befallen you? It is well; for all that befalls you is an ordained part in the weaving of the destiny of all things from the beginning. In sum, life is short. Make the best of the present in reason and in justice. Be sober in your relaxation.

27. The Universe is either an ordered whole or a confusion. But, although a mixture of phenomena, it is certainly an ordered whole. Or, do you think that there can be order in you and confusion in the Universe, and that too when all things, though diffused and separated, are all in sympathy, one with another?

---

28. Consider the deformity of these characters: the black or malicious, the effeminate, the savage, the beastly, the childish, the brutish, the stupid, the false, the ribald, the knavish, the tyrannical.

---

29. He is a foreigner, and not a citizen of the world, who knows not what the world contains; and he, too, who knows not what happens in it. He is a deserter who flies from the reason that rules this polity. He is blind, whose intellectual eye is closed. He is a beggar, who needs the gifts of others, and has not from himself all that is necessary for life. He is an excrescence on the scheme of things, who withdraws and separates himself from the reasoned constitution of the nature in which he shares, by discontent with what befalls. That same nature which produces

this event produced you. He is the seditious citizen who separates his particular soul from the one soul of all reasonable beings.

---

30. One acts the philosopher without a coat, another without books, a third half-naked. Says one, "I have not bread, and yet I hold to reason." Says another, "I have not even the spiritual food of instruction, and yet I hold to it."

---

31. Love the art which you have learned, humble though it be, and in it find your recreation. And spend the remainder of your life as one who with all his heart commits his concerns to the Gods, and neither acts the tyrant nor the slave to any of mankind.

---

32. Recall, for example, the age of Vespasian. It is as the spectacle of our own time. You will see men marrying, bringing up children, sick and dying, warring and feasting, trading and farming. You will see men flattering, obstinate in their own will, suspecting, plotting, wishing for the death

of others, repining at fortune, courting mistresses, hoarding treasure, pursuing consulships and kingdoms. Yet all that life is spent and gone. Come down to Trajan's days. Again, all is the same; and again, that life, too, is dead. Consider, likewise, the records of other times and nations, and see how, after their fit of eagerness, all quickly fell, and were resolved into the elements. But most of all, remember those whom you yourself have known, men who were distracted about vain things, men who neglected the course which suited their own nature, neither holding fast to it nor finding their contentment there. And, herein, forget not that care is to be bestowed on any enterprise only in proportion to its proper worth. For if you keep this in mind you will not be disheartened from over concern with things of less account.

---

33. The familiar phrases of old days are now strange and obsolete; and, likewise, the names of such as were once much celebrated now sound strangely in our ears. Camillus, Caeso, Volesus, Leonnatus; after them Scipio and Cato; lastly, Augustus, Hadrian, and Antonine—all are forgotten. All things hasten to an end, shall speedily seem old fables, and then be buried in

oblivion. This I say of those who have shone with the brightness of their fame. The rest of men, as soon as they expire, are unknown and forgotten. What, then, is it to be remembered forever? A wholly empty thing. For what should we be zealous? For this alone, that our souls be just, our actions unselfish, our speech ever sincere, and our disposition such as may cheerfully embrace whatever happens, seeing it to be inevitable, familiar, and sprung from the same source and origin as we ourselves.

34. Willingly resign yourself to Clotho, permitting her to spin her thread of what yarn she may.

35. All things are for a day, both what remembers and what is remembered.

36. Observe continually that all things exist in change; and keep this thought ever with you, that Nature loves nothing more than changing what things now are, and making others like them. For what now is, is in a manner the seed

of what shall be. Therefore, conceive not that that alone is seed which is cast into the earth or the womb, for that is the thought of ignorance.

---

37. You are presently to die, and yet you have not attained to simplicity or calm, or to disbelief that you can be hurt by things external. You have not learned to be kindly to all men, or to count just dealing the whole of wisdom.

---

38. Scan closely that which governs men; see what are their cares, and what they pursue or shun.

---

39. That which is evil for you exists not in the soul of another; nor in any change or alteration of the body which surrounds you. Where, then, is it? It lies in that part of you by which you apprehend what evil is. Stay the apprehension, and all is well. And though the poor body to which it is so closely bound be cut and burned, though it suppurates or mortifies, yet let the apprehension remain inactive; that is, let it

judge nothing either bad or good which can happen equally to the bad man and to the good. For that which befalls equally him who lives in accord, and him who lives in discord with Nature, can neither be natural nor unnatural.

---

40. Ever consider this Universe as one living being, with one material substance and one spirit. Observe how all things are referred to the one intelligence of this being; how all things act on one impulse; how all things are concurrent causes of all others; and how all things are connected and intertwined.

---

41. "Thou art a poor soul, saddled with a corpse," said Epictetus.

---

42. There is no evil for things which subsist in change; and there can be no good for things which subsist without it.

Time is a river, a violent torrent of things coming into being. Each one, as soon as it has appeared, is swept away: it is succeeded by another which is swept away in its turn.

All that happens is as natural and familiar as a rose in spring, or fruit in summer. Such are disease and death, calumny and treachery, and all else which gives fools joy or sorrow.

Consequents follow antecedents by virtue of a special and necessary connection. This relation is not that which exists in a mere enumeration of independent things, and depends merely on some arbitrary convention. It is a rational relationship. And just as things now existing are ranged harmoniously together, so those which come into existence display no bare succession, but a wonderful harmony with what preceded.

Remember always the sayings of Heraclitus: that the death of earth is to become water, the death of water to become air, and the death of air to become fire; and so conversely. Remember in what a case he is who forgets whither the way leads: that men are frequently at variance with their close and constant companion, the reason which rules all: that men count strange that which they meet every day: that we should neither act nor speak as though in slumber, although even in slumber we seem to act and speak; nor yet like children learning from their parents, with a mere acceptance of everything just as we are told it.

---

47. If some God were to inform you that you must die tomorrow, or the next day at farthest, you would take little concern whether it was to be tomorrow or the next day; that is if you were not the most miserable of cowards. For how small is the difference? Wherefore, account it of no great moment whether you die after many years or tomorrow.

---

48. Constantly consider how many physicians are dead and gone, who frequently knitted their brows over their patients; how many astrologers, who foretold the deaths of others with great

ostentation of their art; how many philosophers, who wrote endlessly on death and immortality; how many warriors, who slew their thousands; and how many tyrants, who used their power of life and death with cruel wantonness, as though they had been immortal. How many whole cities, if I may so speak, are dead: Helice and Pompeii and Herculaneum, and others past counting. Tell over next all those you have known, one after the other: think how one buried his fellow, then lay dead himself, to be buried by a third. And all this within a little time. In sum, look upon human things, and behold how short-lived and how vile they are; mucus yesterday, tomorrow ashes or pickled carrion. Spend, then, the fleeting remnant of your time in a spirit that accords with Nature, and depart contentedly. So, the olive falls when it is grown ripe, blessing the ground from whence it sprung, and thankful to the tree that bore it.

---

49. Be like a promontory against which the waves are always breaking. It stands fast, and stills the waters that rage around it. "Wretched am I," says one, "that this has befallen me." "Nay," say you, "happy am I who, though this has befallen

me, can still remain without sorrow, neither broken by the present nor dreading the future." The like might have befallen any one; but everyone would not have endured it unpained. Why, then, should we dwell more on the misfortune of the incident than on the felicity of such strength of mind? Can you call that a misfortune for a man which is not a miscarriage of his nature? And can you call anything a miscarriage of his nature which is not contrary to its purpose? You have learned its purpose, have you not? Then does this accident debar you from justice, magnanimity, prudence, wisdom, caution, truth, honor, freedom, and all else in the possession of which man's nature finds its full estate? Remember, therefore, for the future, upon all occasions of sorrow, to use the maxim: this thing is not misfortune, but to bear it bravely is good fortune.

---

50. It is a vulgar meditation, and yet very effectual for enabling us to despise death, to consider the fate of those who have been most earnestly tenacious of life, and enjoyed it longest. Wherein is their gain greater than that of those who died before their time? They are all lying dead somewhere or other. Cadicianus, Fabius, Julian,

Lepidus, and their fellows, saw the corpses of multitudes carried to the grave, and then themselves were carried thither. In sum, how small was the difference of time, spent painfully amid what troubles, among what worthless men, and in how mean a carcass! Think it not a thing of value. Rather look back into the eternity that gapes behind, and forward into the other abyss of immensity. Compared with such infinity, small is the difference between a life of three days and one of three ages like Nestor's.

Run ever the short way. The short way is the way according to Nature. Therefore, speak and act according to the soundest rule; for this resolution will free you from much toil and warring, and from all artful management and

THE FIFTH BOOK

In the morning, when you find yourself unwilling to rise, have this thought at hand: I arise to the proper business of man, and shall I repine at setting about that work for which I was born and brought into the world? Am I equipped for nothing but to lie among the bedclothes and keep warm? "But," you say, "it is more pleasant so." Is pleasure, then, the object of your being, and not action, and the exercise of your powers? Do you not see the smallest plants, the little sparrows, the ants, the spiders, the bees, all doing their part, and working for order in the Universe, as far as in them lies? And will you refuse the part in this design which is laid on man? Will you not pursue the course which accords with your own nature? You say, "I must have rest." Assuredly; but nature appoints a measure for rest, just as for eating and drinking. In rest you go beyond these limits, and beyond what is enough; but in action you do not fill the measure, and remain well within your powers. You do not love yourself; if you did, you would love your nature and its purpose. Others, who love the art that they have made their own, exhaust themselves with laboring at it unwashed and unfed. But you honor your own nature less than the carver honors his carving, less than the dancer honors his dancing, the miser his gold, or the vain man his empty fame. These men, when desire takes them, count food and sleep well lost if they can better realize the object of their longings; and shall the pursuit of the common good seem less precious in your eyes and worthy of a lesser zeal?

---

2. How easy it is to thrust away and blot out each impression that is disturbing and unfit; and forthwith to enjoy perfect tranquility.

---

3. Judge no speech or action unworthy of you which is consistent with nature. Be not dissuaded by any consequent criticism or censure from others; but, if the speech or action be honorable, judge yourself worthy to say or do it. Those who

criticize you have their own conscience and their own motives. These you are not to regard, but follow a straight course, guided by your own nature and the nature of the Universe, both of which point the same way.

---

4. I walk the way which is Nature's, until at last I shall fall and be at rest; breathing out my breath into the air wherefrom I daily drew it, falling on that earth whence my father drew his seed, my mother her blood, and my nurse the milk which nourished me; on that earth which has given me my daily food and drink through all these years, which sustains my footsteps, and bears with me—her manifold abuser.

---

5. Men cannot admire you for your shrewdness. Be it so. But there is many another quality of which you cannot say, "It is not in me." Display these; they are wholly in your power. Be sincere, be dignified, be painstaking; scorn pleasure, repine not at fate, need little; be kind and frank; love not exaggeration and vain talk; strive after greatness. Do you not see how many virtues you might show, of which you are yet content to fall

short, though you have not the excuse that they are absent, or that you are unfit for them? Are you driven by some want in your equipment to be querulous, to be miserly, to be a flatterer, to reproach your body with your own faults, to cringe to others, to be vainglorious, to have all this restlessness in your soul? No, by the Gods, you might have escaped these vices long ago. All your fault, then, is that you are somewhat slow and dull of comprehension. This you should strive to correct by exercise; neither neglecting your dullness nor taking a mean pleasure in it.

Some men, when they have done you a favor, are very ready to reckon up the obligation they have conferred. Others, again, are not so forward in their claims, but yet in their minds consider you their debtor, and well know the value of what they have done. A third sort seem to be unconscious of their service. They are like the vine, which produces its clusters and is satisfied when it has yielded its proper fruit. The horse when he has run his course, the hound when he has followed the track, the bee when it has made its honey, and the man when he has done good to others, make no noisy boast of it, but set out to do the same once more, as the vine in its season produces its new clusters again. "Should we, then, be among those who in a manner know not what they do?" Assuredly. "But this very thing implies intelligence; for it is a property of the unselfish man to perceive that he is acting unselfishly, and, surely, to wish his fellow also to perceive it." True, but if you misapprehend my saying, you will enter the ranks of those of whom I spoke before. They, too, are led astray by specious reasonings. But if you have the will to understand what my principle truly means, fear not that in following it you will neglect the duty of unselfishness.

7. This is a prayer of the Athenians: "Rain, rain, dear Zeus, on the plains and ploughlands of the Athenians." Man should either not pray at all, or pray after this frank and simple fashion.

8. Just as one says that Aesculapius has prescribed a course of riding for someone, or the cold bath, or walking barefooted; so, it may be said that the guiding Mind prescribes for a man, disease, or mutilation, or losses, or the like. "Prescribed," in the first case, means that such treatment was enjoined on the patient as might coincide with

the needs of his health: in the second case it means that each man's fortune is appointed to coincide with the purposes of fate. Now, the very word "coincidence" implies something like that correspondence of squared stones in a wall or pyramid, which workmen speak of when they fit them together in some structure. All things are united in one bond of harmony; and just as all existing bodies go to make the visible world what it is, so destiny, as the general cause, is compounded of all particular causes. The most unphilosophical grasp my meaning, for they say, "Fate gave this to so-and-so: this was appointed or prescribed for him." Let us, then, receive the decrees of Fate as we receive the prescriptions of Aesculapius. He prescribes many things for us, and some of them are harsh medicines. Yet we obey him gladly in the hope of health. Conceive therefore that, for Nature, the doing of her work and the fulfilling of her purposes are, as it were, her health; and welcome all that happens, even should it seem hard fortune, because it tends to the health of the Universe, and to the prosperity and felicity of Zeus. He would not have brought this or that on any man did it not contribute to the good of the whole, nor does any part of Nature's system bring aught to pass which suits not with her government. For two reasons, then, you should content yourself with what befalls you. The first is, that it was created and ordained for you, and was in a manner related to you from the beginning, in the weaving of all destinies from the great first causes. The second is, that even what happens severally to each man contributes to the well-being and prosperity of the Mind which governs all things, and, indeed, even to its continued existence. For the whole is maimed if you break in the slightest degree this continuous connection, whether of parts or causes. And this you are doing your best to break and to destroy whenever you repine at fate.

9. Fret not, neither despond nor be disheartened, if it be not always possible for you to act according to your principles of perfection. If you are beaten off, return again to the effort, and content yourself that your conduct is generally such as becomes a man. Love the good to which you return; and come back to Philosophy, not as one who comes to a master, but as one whose eyes ache recurs to sponge and egg, as another has recourse to plasters, or a third to fomentation. And thus, you will make no empty show of obeying reason; but find that it gives you rest. Remember that Philosophy demands no more than what your nature requires. But you are wont to desire other things which accord not with your nature. "For what," you say, "can be

more delightful than such things?" Is not this the very snare which Pleasure sets for us? Yet consider if magnanimity, frankness, simplicity, kindness, and piety be not even greater delights. And what is sweeter than wisdom itself, when you are conscious of security and felicity in your powers of apprehension and reason?

---

10. The natures of things are so covered up from us, that to many philosophers, and these no mean ones, all things seem incomprehensible. The Stoics themselves own that it is difficult to comprehend anything with certainty. All our assent is inconsistent, for where is the consistent man? Consider, too, the objects of our knowledge: how transitory are they, and how mean! How often they are in the possession of the debauchee, of the harlot, of the robber! Review again the morals of your contemporaries: it is scarcely possible to tolerate the best mannered among them; not to say that a man can scarcely tolerate himself. Amid such darkness and filth, in this perpetual flux of substance, of time, of motion, and of things moved, I can perceive nothing worthy of esteem or of desire. On the contrary, we should comfort ourselves as we await our natural dissolution

and not be vexed at the delay, but find rest in these thoughts: first, that nothing can befall us which is not in accord with the nature of all things; second, that it is always in our power not to do anything against the divine spirit within us: to this no force can compel us.

---

11. To what end am I using my soul? Let me examine myself as to this on all occasions, and consider what is passing now in that part of me which men call the ruler of the rest. Let me think, too, whose is the soul that I have. Is it a child's? Is it a youth's, a timorous woman's, or a tyrant's; the soul of a tame beast or of a savage one?

---

12. Of what value the things are which the many account good you may judge from this: If a man has conceived certain things, such as prudence, temperance, justice, or courage, to be good in the real sense, he cannot, while he is of this mind, readily listen to the traditional gibe about a superabundance of good things. It will not fit the case. But when he has in mind things which seem good in the eyes of the multitude, he is perfectly willing to hear and accept as

quite appropriate the raillery of the comic poet. Thus, even the ordinary mind perceives the difference. For if this were not so, we would not in the first case repudiate the jest as offensive, nor would we salute it as a happy witticism when applied to wealth or to the opulence which produces luxury and ostentation. Proceed then, and put the question whether these things are to be valued and esteemed good of which we have such an opinion that we may aptly say of their possessor: "He has so many possessions about him that he has no place wherein to ease himself."

---

13. I consist of a formal and a material element. Neither of these two shall die and fade into nothingness, since neither came into being out of nothing. Every part of me, then, will be transformed and ranged again in some part of the Universe. That part of the Universe will itself be transmuted into another part, and so on for all time coming. By some such change as this I came into being, likewise my progenitors, and so back from all time past. There is no objection to this theory, even though the world be governed by determined cycles of revolution.

14. Reason, and the art of thinking, are powers which are complete in themselves, and in their special processes. They start from their own internal principle, and proceed to their appointed end. Such mental acts are called right, to indicate that the course of thought is right or straight.

---

15. Nothing should be said to be part of a man which is not part of his human nature. Things that are not part of his essence cannot be required of him, and have no part in the promise or the fulfilment of his nature. Therefore, in such things lies neither the end of man nor the good which crowns that end. Moreover, if anything were really part of a man, it would not be proper for him to despise it or revolt against it, nor would he be praiseworthy who made himself independent thereof. If nonessential things were indeed good, he could be no good man who stinted himself in the use of them; but, as we see, the more a man goes without them, and the more he endures the want of them, the better a man he is.

16. The character of your most frequent impressions will be the character of your mind. The soul takes color from its impressions, therefore steep it in such thoughts as these: Wherever a man can live, he can live well. A man can live in a court; therefore, he can live well there. Again, everything works towards that for which it was created, and that to which anything works is its end; and in the end of everything is to be found the advantage and the good of it. Now, for reasoning beings, Society is the highest good, for it has long since been proved that we were brought into the world to be social. Nay, was it not manifest that the inferior kinds were formed for the superior, and the superior for each other? Now, the animate is superior to the inanimate, and beings that reason to those that only live.

---

17. To pursue impossibilities is madness; and it is impossible that the wicked should not act in some such way as this.

---

18. Nothing can befall any man which he is not fitted by nature to bear. The like events befall others, and either through ignorance that the event has happened, or from ostentation of

magnanimity, they stand firm and unhurt by them. Strange then that ignorance or ostentation should have more strength than wisdom!

---

19. Material things cannot touch the soul at all, nor have any access to it: neither can they bend or move it. The soul is bent or moved by itself alone, and remodels all things that present themselves from without in accordance with whatever judgment it adopts within.

---

20. In one respect man is nearest and dearest to me; in so far, that is, as I must do good to him and bear with him. But in so far as some men obstruct me in my natural activities, man enters the class of things indifferent to me, no less than the sun, the wind, or the wild beast. By these indeed some special action may be impeded, but no interference with my purpose or with my inward disposition can come from them, thanks to my exceptive and modifying powers. For the mind can convert and change everything that impedes its activity into matter for its action; hindrance in its work becomes its real help, and every obstruction makes for its progress.

21. Reverence that which is most excellent in the Universe, and the most excellent is that which employs all things and rules all. Likewise reverence that which is most excellent in yourself. It is of the same nature as the former, for it is that which employs all else that is in you, and that by which your whole life is ordered.

---

22. That which harms not the city cannot harm the citizen. Apply this rule whenever you have the idea that you are hurt. If the state be not hurt by this, neither am I harmed, and if the state be hurt, we should not be wrathful with him who hurt it. Consider where lay his oversight.

---

23. Consider frequently how swiftly things that exist or are coming into existence are swept by and carried away. Their substance is as a river perpetually flowing; their actions are in continual change, and their causes subject to ten thousand alterations. Scarcely anything is stable, and the vast eternities of past and future in which all things are swallowed up are close upon us on both hands. Is he not then a fool who is puffed up with success in the things of this world, or is

distracted, or worried, as if he were in a time of trouble likely to endure for long.

---

24. Keep in mind the universe of being in which your part is exceeding small, the universe of time of which a brief and fleeting moment is assigned to you; the destiny of things, and how infinitesimal your share therein.

---

25. Does another wrong me? Let him look to that. His character and his actions are his own. So much is in my present possession as is dispensed to me by the nature of things, and I act as my own nature now bids me.

---

26. Let the leading and ruling part of your soul stand unmoved by the stirrings of the flesh, whether gentle or rude. Let it not commingle with them, but keep itself apart, and confine these passions to their proper bodily parts; and if they rise into the soul by any sympathy with the body to which it is united, then we must not attempt to resist the sensation, seeing that it is of our nature;

but let not the soul, for its part, add thereto the conception that the sensation is good or bad.

---

27. Live with the Gods. And he lives with the Gods who continually displays to them his soul, living in satisfaction with its lot, and doing the will of the inward spirit, a portion of his own divinity which Zeus has given to every man for a ruler and a guide. This is the intelligence, the reason that abides in us all.

---

28. Are you angry with one whose armpits smell or whose breath is foul? What is the use? His mouth or his armpits are so, and the consequence must follow. But, you say, man is a reasonable being, and could by attention discern in what he offends. Very well, you too have reason. Use your reason to move his; instruct, admonish him. If he listens, you will cure him, and there will be no reason for anger. You are neither actor nor harlot.

---

29. As you intend to live at your going, so you can live here. But, if men do not permit you, then

depart from life, yet so as if no misfortune had befallen you. If my house be smoky, I go out, and where is the great matter? So long as no such trouble drives me out, I remain at my will, and no one will prevent me from acting as I will. And my will is the will of a reasonable and social being.

30. The intelligence of the Universe is social. It has therefore made the inferior orders for the sake of the superior; and has suited the superior beings for one another. You see how it has subordinated, and coordinated, and distributed to each according to its merit, and engaged the nobler beings to a mutual agreement and unanimity.

---

31. How have you behaved towards the Gods, towards your parents, your brothers, your wife, your children, your teachers, those who reared you, your friends, your intimates, your slaves? Can it be said that you have ever acted towards all of them in the spirit of the line:

He wrought no harshness, spoke no unkind word?

Recollect all you have passed through, all that you have had strength to bear. Your life is now a tale that is told, and your service is all discharged. Recall the fair sights you have seen, the pleasures and the pains you have despised, the so-called glory that you have foregone, the unkindly men to whom you have shown kindness.

---

32. How is it that unskilled and ignorant souls disturb the skillful and intelligent? What, I ask, is the skillful and intelligent soul? It is that which knows the beginning and the end, and the reason which pervades all being, and by determined cycles rules the Universe for all time.

---

33. In a little space you will be only ashes and dry bones and a name, perhaps not even that. A name is but so much empty sound and echo, and the things which are so much prized in life are empty, mean, and rotten. We are as puppies that snap at one another, as children that quarrel, laugh, and presently weep again. But integrity, modesty, justice, and truth:

Up from the wide-wayed earth have soared to heaven.

What then should detain you here? Things sensible are ever changing and unstable. The senses are dull and easily deceived. The poor soul itself is a mere exhalation from blood. Fame in such a world is a thing of naught. What then? You await calmly extinction or transformation, whichever it may be. And till the fulness of the time become what is to suffice you? What else than a life spent in fearing and praising the Gods, and in the practice of benevolence, toleration and forbearance towards men? And whatsoever lies beyond the bounds of flesh and breath, remember that it is neither yours nor in your power.

---

34. A prosperous life may be yours if only you can take the right path, and keep to it in all you think or do. Two advantages are common to Gods, to men, and to every rational soul. In the first place, nothing external to themselves has power to hinder them. In the second, their happiness lies in having mind and conduct disposed to justice, and in the power to make that the end of all desire.

35. If the fault be not my sin, nor a consequence of it, if there be no damage to the common good, why am I perturbed about it? Wherein is the harm to the common good?

---

36. Be not incautiously carried away by sentiment, but aid him that needs it according to your power and his desert. If his need be of the things which are indifferent, think not that he is harmed thereby, for so to think is an evil habit. But as, in the Comedy, the old man begs to have his foster child's top for a keepsake, though he knows well that it is a top and nothing more, so should you act also in the affairs of life.

You mount the rostra and cry aloud, "O man, have you forgotten what is the real value of what you seek?" "No, but the many are keen in their pursuit of it." "Are you then to be a fool because they are?"

In whatever case I had been left I could have made my fortune: for what is it to make a fortune but to confer good things upon one's self; and true good things are a worthy frame of mind, worthy impulses, worthy actions.

THE SIXTH BOOK

1. The substance of the Universe is docile and pliable. The mind which governs it has in itself no source of evildoing. It has no malice: it does no ill, and nothing is hurt by it. By its guidance all things come to be, and fulfill their being.

---

2. Act the part which is worthy of you, regarding not whether you be stiff with cold or comfortably warm; whether you be drowsy or refreshed with sleep; whether you be in good report or bad; whether you be dying or upon some other business. For death also is one piece of the business of life, and, here as elsewhere, it is enough to do well what comes to our hand.

Look within. Let not the proper quality or value of anything escape you.

All that exists will very speedily change; by rarefaction, if all substance be one; otherwise by dispersion.

The guiding mind knows what its own condition is, how, and upon what matter its work is done.

The best revenge is not to copy him that wronged you.

Find your sole delight and recreation in proceeding from one unselfish action to another, with God ever in mind.

8. The ruling part of you is that which rouses and steers itself, making itself what it wishes to be, and making all that happens take such appearance as it will.

---

9. All things are accomplished according to the will of universal nature. There is no other nature to influence them which either comprchends the former from without, or is contained within it, or exists externally, and independent of it.

---

10. The Universe is either a confusion raveled and unraveled again, or else a unity compact of order and forethought. If it be the former, why should I wish to linger amid this aimless chaos and confusion, or have any further care than "how to become earth again?" Nay, why am I disturbed at all? Dissolution will overtake me, do what I please. But, if the latter be the case, I adore the Ruler of all things, I stand firm, and put my trust in him.

11. Whenever your situation forces trouble upon you, return quickly to yourself, and interrupt the rhythm of life no longer than you are compelled. Your grasp of the harmony will grow surer by continual recurrence to it.

---

12. Had you at one time both a stepmother and a mother, you would respect the former, yet you would be more constantly in your mother's company. Your court and your philosophy are stepmother and mother to you. Return then frequently to your true mother, and recreate yourself with her. Her consolation can make the court seem bearable to you, and you to it.

---

13. Keep these thoughts for meats and eatables: This that is before me is the dead carcass of a fish, a fowl, a hog. This Falernian is but a little grape juice. Think of your purple robes as sheep's wool stained in the blood of a shellfish. Such conceptions, which touch reality so near, and set forth the sum and substance of these objects, are powerful indeed to display to us their despicable value. In this spirit we should act throughout life; and when things of great apparent worth present themselves, we should strip them naked,

view their meanness, and cast aside the glowing description which makes them seem so glorious. Vanity is a great sophist, and most imposes on us when we believe ourselves to be busy about the noblest ends. Remember the saying of Crates about Xenocrates himself.

---

14. Most objects of vulgar admiration may be referred to certain general classes. There are, first, those which hold together by cohesion or by some organic unity, such as stone, timber, figs, vines or olives. The things which men, a shade more reasonable, admire are referred to the class which possesses animal life such as is seen in flocks and herds. When man's taste is still more cultured his admiration turns to things which can show a rational intelligence. But he admires this intelligence not as a universal principle, but only so far as he finds it expressed in art or industry, or, indeed, sometimes merely so far as it is exhibited by his retinue of artist slaves. But he who values rational intelligence as a universal thing, and as a social force, will care nothing for these other objects of admiration. He will, above all things, strive to preserve his own mind in all its rational and social instincts and activities; and to this end he will cooperate with any of his kind.

15. Some things hasten into being. Some hasten to be no more. Even as a thing is born some part of it is already dead. Flux and change are constantly renewing the world, just as the unbroken flow of time ever presents to us some new portion of eternity. In this vast river, on whose bosom there is no tarrying, what is there among the things that sweep by us that is worth the prizing? It is as if a man grew fond of one among a passing flight of sparrows, when already it had vanished from his sight. Our life itself is much like a vapor of the blood or a drawing in of air. Our momentary actions of inhalation and exhalation are one in kind with that whole power of breathing which, yesterday or the day before, we received at birth, and which we must restore again to the source from whence we drew it.

---

16. It is a small privilege to transpire like plants, or even to breathe as cattle or wild beasts do. To feel the impressions of sense, to be swayed like puppets by passion, to herd together and to live by bread; all this is no great thing. There is nothing here superior to our power of discharging our superfluous food. What, then, is of value? To be received with clapping of hands? No. Neither, therefore, is the applause

of tongues more valuable, for the praises of the multitude are naught but the idle clapping of tongues. Dismiss the vanity called fame, and what remains to be prized? This, I think: in all things to act, or to restrain yourself from action, as best suits the particular structure of your nature. This is the end of all arts and studies, for every art aims at making what it produces well adapted to the work for which it was designed. The gardener, the vine dresser, the horse breaker, the dog trainer all try for this; and what else is the aim of all education and teaching? Here, then, is what you may truly value: this well won, you will seek for nothing more. Will you, then, cease valuing the multitude of other things? If you do not, you will never attain to freedom, self-sufficiency, or tranquility. You cannot escape envying, suspecting, and striving against those who have the power to deprive you of your cherished objects, nor plotting against men who are in possession of that on which you set your heart. The man who lacks any of these things must, of necessity, be distracted, and be forever complaining against the Gods. But reverence and respect for your own intelligence will bring you to agreement with yourself, into concord with mankind, and into harmony with the Gods, whom you will praise for all their good gifts and guidance.

17. Upward, downward, round and round run the courses of the elements. But the course of virtue is like none of these; it follows a diviner path, well directed in a way that is hard for us to understand.

18. Strange are the ways of men! They can speak no good word of the contemporaries with whom they live; yet they count it a great thing to gain the praises of a posterity whom they never saw nor shall see. As well might we grieve because we cannot hear the praises of our ancestors.

who is plotting against us. We are on our guard against him, it is true, but not as against an enemy or a suspected person. In all good humor we simply keep out of his way. Let us thus behave in other affairs of life, and overlook the many injuries which are done to us, as it were, by our antagonists in the gymnasium of the world. As I said, we may keep out of their way, but without suspicion or hatred.

---

21. If anyone can convince or shew me that I am wrong in thought or deed, I will gladly change. It is truth that I seek; and truth never yet hurt any man. What does hurt is persistence in error or in ignorance.

---

22. I do my duty, and for the rest am not distracted by anything which is inanimate or irrational, or which has lost or ignores the proper way.

---

23. Use the brute creation, and also all material things, in the spirit of magnanimity and freedom which becomes him who has reason in using that

which has it not. Towards men, who have reason, act in a social spirit. In every business call the Gods to aid you, nor trouble how long this business shall endure; three hours spent therein may suffice you.

---

24. Alexander of Macedon and his muleteer, when they died, were in a like condition. They were either alike resumed into the seminal source of all things, or alike dispersed among the atoms.

---

25. Consider all the many things, both physical and spiritual, that are doing within each of us at the very same instant of time; and you will wonder the less at the far greater multitudes of things, even all that is, which exist together in the one-and-all which we call the Universe.

---

26. Should someone ask you how the name Antoninus is written, would you not carefully pronounce to him each one of the letters? Should he then begin an angry dispute about it, would you also grow angry, and not rather

mildly count over the several letters to him? Thus, in life remember that each duty is made up of a number of elements. We should observe all these calmly; and, without anger at those who are angry with us, we should set about accomplishing the task which lies before us.

---

27. Is it not cruel to restrain men from pursuing what appears to be their own advantage? And yet, in a manner, you deny them this liberty when you shew anger at their errors. Men are assuredly attracted to what seems to be their own advantage. "Yes," you say, "but it is not their advantage." Instruct them, then, and make this evident to them, but without anger.

---

28. Death is the cessation of the sensual impressions, of the impulses of the passions, of the questionings of reason, and of the servitude to the flesh.

---

29. It is shame and dishonor that, in any man's life, the soul should faint from its duty while the body still holds out.

See to it that you fall not into Caesarism: avoid that stain, for it may come to you. Guard your simplicity, your goodness, your sincerity, your dignity, your reticence, your love of justice, your piety, your kindliness, your affection for your kin, and your constancy to your duty. Endeavour earnestly to continue such as philosophy would make you. Reverence the Gods, and help mankind. Life is short, and the one fruit of it in this world is a pure mind and unselfish conduct. Be in all things the disciple of Antonine. Imitate his resolute constancy to rational action, his level equability, his godliness, his serenity of countenance, his sweetness of temper, his contempt of vainglory, his keen attempts to comprehend things. Remember how he never quitted any subject till he had thoroughly examined it and understood it, and how he bore with those who blamed him unjustly, without making any angry retort: how he was never in a hurry; how he discouraged calumny; how closely he scanned the manners and actions of men; how cautious he was in reproaching any man; how free from fear, suspicion, or sophistry; how little contented him in the matter of house, furniture, dress, food, servants; how patient he was of labor, and how slow to anger. So abstemious was his life that he could hold out until evening without relieving himself, except at the usual hour. What a firm and loyal friend he was; how patient of frank opposition to his opinions; how glad if anyone could set him right! How religious he was, and yet how free from superstition! Follow in his steps that your last hour may find you with a conscience as easy as his.

---

31. Sober yourself, recall your senses. Shake sleep from you, and know that it was a dream that troubled you; and, now that you are broad awake again, regard the waking world as you did the dream.

---

32. I am made up of a frail body and a soul. To the body all things are indifferent, because it cannot distinguish them; and to the mind all things are indifferent also which arise not from its own activities. All these are indeed in its own power, but it is concerned with only such of them as are present. Its past and future activities are indifferent to it now.

33. No toil for hand or foot is against Nature, so long as it is proper for hand or foot to do. No more, then, is toil contrary to the nature of man, as man, so long as he is doing work appointed for man to do; and if it be not contrary to his nature it cannot be evil for him.

34. How many are the pleasures that have been enjoyed by robbers, rakes, parricides, and tyrants!

35. Do you not see how common artificers, though they may humor the public to a certain extent, cling to the rules of their art, and cannot endure to depart from them? Is it not grievous, then, that the architect and the physician should shew greater respect for the rules of their several professions, than man shews for his own reason, which he possesses in common with the Gods?

36. Asia and Europe are mere corners of the Universe: the whole sea is but a drop, Athos a clod. All the present is but an instant in eternity. All things are small, changeable, and fleeting. Everything proceeds from the universal intelligence, either directly or as a consequence. Thus, the jaws of lions, poisons, all evil things such as thorns or mire, are the consequences of the grand and the beautiful. Do not, then, imagine that they are foreign to that which you revere, but consider well the source of all things.

---

37. He who has seen the present has seen all that either has been from all eternity, or will be to all eternity, for all things are alike in kind and form.

---

38. Consider frequently the connection of all things in the Universe, and their relation to each other. All things are in a manner intermingled with one another, and are, therefore, mutually friendly. For one thing comes in due order after another, by virtue of local movements, and of the harmony and unity of the whole.

39. Adapt yourself to the things which your destiny has given you: love those with whom it is your lot to live, and love them with sincere affection.

---

40. A tool, an instrument, a utensil, is in good case when it is fit for its proper work: yet its maker remains not by it. But within the organisms of Nature there remains and resides the power which made them. You ought, therefore, to reverence this power the more, believing that if you act in deference to its will, all will happen to you in reason; for so in reason the Universe ranges all.

---

41. Whenever we imagine that anything which lies not in our power is good or evil for us, if the evil befalls us or if we miss the good, we inevitably blame the Gods, and hate the men who are, or whom we suspect to be, the cause of our disaster or our loss. Our solicitude about such things leads to much injustice; but if we judge only the things that are in our power to be good or evil, there is no reason left for accusing the Gods or for hating men.

42. We are all cooperating in one great work, some with knowledge and understanding, others ignorantly and without design. It is in this sense, I think, that Heraclitus says that men are working even while they sleep, working together in all that is being done in the Universe. Each works in a different way; and even those contribute abundantly who murmur and try to oppose and to frustrate the course of nature. The world has need even of such as these. It remains then for you to make sure which is the class in which you rank yourself. The presiding mind will assuredly use you to good purpose one way or other; and will enlist you among its laborers and fellow workers. But see to it that the part that falls to you lie not in the vulgar comic passage of the play, of which Chrysippus has spoken.

---

43. Does the sun pretend to perform the work of the rain, or Aesculapius that of Ceres? What of the several stars? Are they not different, yet all jointly working for the same end?

44. If the Gods took counsel about me and what should befall me, doubtless then-counsel was good. It is difficult to imagine Gods wanting in forethought, and what could move them to do me wilfull harm? What advantage would thence accrue, either to themselves or to the Universe which is their special care? If they have not taken counsel about me in particular, they certainly have done so about the common interest of the Universe, and I therefore should accept cheerfully and contentedly the fate which is the outcome of their ordinance. If, indeed, they take no counsel about anything (which it is impious to believe), then let us quit our sacrifices, our prayers, and our oaths, and all acts of devotion which we now perform as if they lived and moved amongst us. But, granting that the Gods take no thought for my affairs, I may still deliberate about myself. It is my business to consider my own interest. Now, each man's interest is that which agrees with the structure of his nature, and my nature is rational and social. As Antoninus, my city and my country is Rome; as a human being it is the world. That alone, then, which profits these two cities can profit me.

45. All that happens to the individual is of profit to the whole. This would suffice. But if you consider closely, you will see that it is also a general truth that all that happens to one man is of profit to the rest of mankind. "Profit" here should be taken in a somewhat general sense, as referring to things indifferent.

---

46. In the amphitheater and other such resorts the same or similar spectacles, continually presented, cloy at last. It is even so in all our experience of life. All things, first and last, are alike, and like derived. When shall the end be?

---

47. Think continually of all the men that are dead and gone, men of every sort and condition, of all manner of pursuits, and of every nation. Return back to Philistion, Phoebus, and Origanion. Pass down to other generations of the dead. We must all change our habitation and go to that place whither so many great orators, so many venerable philosophers, Heraclitus, Pythagoras, Socrates, and so many heroes have gone before, and so many generals and princes have followed. Add to

these Eudoxus, Hipparchus, Archimedes, and other keen, great, laborious, cunning and arrogant spirits; yes, such as have wittily derided this fading mortal life which is but for a day, as did Menippus and his brethren. Consider that all these are long since in their graves. And wherein here is the harm for them; or even for men whose names are not remembered? The one precious thing in life is to spend it in a steady course of truth and justice, with kindliness even for the false and the unjust.

---

48. When you would cheer your heart, consider the several excellencies of those that live around you. Consider the activity of one, the modesty of another, the generosity of a third, and the other virtues of the rest. Nothing rejoices the heart so much as instances, the more the better, of goodness manifested in the characters of those around us. Let us, therefore, have such instances ever present for reflection.

---

49. Are you grieved that you weigh only these few pounds, and not three hundred? If not, is there greater reason to sorrow if you live only so many

years and no longer? You are satisfied with your allotted quantity of matter; content yourself then likewise with the span of time appointed you.

---

50. Try to persuade men to agree with you; but whether they agree or not, pursue the course you have marked out when the principles of justice point that way. Should one oppose you by force, act with resignation, and shew not that you are hurt, use the obstruction for the exercise of some other virtue, and remember that your purpose involved the reservation that you were not to aim at impossibilities. What, after all, was your aim? To make some good effort such as this. Well, then, you have succeeded, even though your first purpose be not accomplished.

---

51. The vainglorious man places his happiness in the action of others. The sensualist finds it in his own sensations. The wise man realizes it in his own work.

52. You have it in your power to form no opinion about this or that, and so to have peace of mind. Things material have no power to form our opinions for us.

---

53. Accustom yourself to attend closely to what is said by others, and as far as possible to penetrate into the mind of the speaker.

---

54. What profits not the swarm profits not the bee.

---

55. If the sailors revile their pilot, or the sick their physician, whom will they follow or obey? And how will the one secure safety to the crew, or the other health to the patients?

---

56. How many who entered the world with me are already departed!

57. To the jaundiced, honey seems bitter; and water is a thing of dread to those bitten by mad dogs. To boys, a ball is a glorious thing. Why, then, am I angry? Has error in the mind less power than a little bile in the jaundiced, or a little poison in him who is bitten?

---

58. No man can prevent you from living according to the plan of your nature; and nothing can befall you which is contrary to the plan of the nature of the Universe.

---

59. Consider what men are; whom they seek to please; what they expect to gain, and how they go about to compass their ends. Think how soon eternity will shroud all things, and how much is already shrouded.

THE SEVENTH BOOK

1. What is vice? It is what you have often seen. In every instance of it, keep in mind that you have often seen the like before. Search up and down; you will find sameness everywhere. Among the events which fill the history of ancient, middle, and present ages; among the things of which our cities and our households are full today, nothing is new, all is familiar and fleeting.

---

2. How can the great principles of life become dead if the impressions which correspond to them be not extinguished? These impressions you may still rekindle. I can always form the proper opinion of this or that; and, if so, why am I disturbed? What is external to my mind is of no

consequence to it. Learn this, and you stand upright; you can always renew your life. See things again as once you saw them, and your life is made new again.

---

3. Your vain concern for shows, for stage plays, for flocks and herds, your little combats, are as bones cast for the contention of puppies, as baits dropped into a fishpond, as the toil of ants and the burdens that they bear, as the scampering of frightened mice, or the antics of puppets jerked by wires. It is then your duty amid all this to stand firm, kindly and not proud, yet to understand that a man's worth is just the worth of that which he pursues.

---

4. In conversation we should give good heed to what is said, and in every enterprise, we should attend to what is done. In the latter case, at once look to the end in view, and, in the former, note the meaning intended.

5. Is my understanding sufficient for this business or not? If it be sufficient, I use it for the work in hand as an instrument given to me by nature. If it be not sufficient, I either give place to one better fitted for the achievement, or, if for some reason this be not a proper course, I do it as best I can, taking the aid of those who, by directing my mind, can accomplish something fit and serviceable for the common good. For all that I do, whether by myself or with the help of others, should be directed solely towards what is fit and useful for the public service.

6. How many of those who were once so mightily acclaimed are delivered up to oblivion? And how many of those who acclaimed them are dead and gone this many a day?

7. Be not ashamed of taking assistance. It is laid upon you to do your part, as on a soldier when the wall is stormed. What, then, if you are lame, and cannot scale the battlements alone, but can with another's help?

Be not troubled about the future. You will come to it, if need be, with the same power to reason, as you use upon your present business.

All things are twined together, in one sacred bond. Scarce is there one thing quite foreign to another. They are all ranged together, and leagued to form the same ordered whole. The Universe, compact of all things, is one; through all things runs one divinity; being is one; and law, which is the reason common to all intelligent creatures; and truth is one as well, that is if there be but one sort of perfection possible to all beings which are of the same nature and partake of the same rational power.

Everything material is soon engulfed in the matter of the whole, and every active cause is swiftly resumed into the Universal reason. The memory of all things is quickly buried in eternity.

In the reasoning being to act according to nature is to act according to reason.

12. Be upright either by nature or by correction.

---

13. In an organic unity, bodily members play the same part as reasoning beings among separate existences, since both are fitted for one joint operation. This thought will come home to you the more vividly if you say often to yourself: "I am a member of the mighty organism which is made up of reasoning beings." If, instead of a member, you say that you are merely a part, you have not as yet attained to a heartfelt love of mankind. As yet you love not well doing for its own sake alone, and you still perform your bare duty, with no thought that you are your own benefactor by the deed.

---

14. From the world without let what will affect whatever parts are subject to such affection. Let the part which suffers complain, if it will, of the suffering. But I, if I admit not that the hap is evil, remain uninjured. Not to admit it is surely in my power.

15. Let anyone say or do what he pleases, I must be a good man. It is just as gold, or emeralds, or purple might say continually: "Let men do or say what they please, I must be an emerald, and retain my luster."

---

16. The soul which rules you vexes not itself. It does not, for example, awake its own fears or arouse its own desires. If another can raise grief or terror in it, let him do so. By its own impressions it will not be led into such emotions.

Let the body take thought, if it can, for itself, lest it suffer anything, and complain when it suffers. The soul, by means of which we experience fear and sorrow, and by means of which, indeed, we receive any impression of these, will admit no suffering. You cannot force it to any such opinion.

The ruling part is, in itself, free from all dependence, unless it makes itself dependent. Similarly, it may be free from all disturbance and obstruction, if it does not disturb and obstruct itself.

17. To have good fortune is to have a good spirit, or a good mind. What do you here, Imagination? Be gone, I say, even as you came. I have no need for you. You came, you say, after your ancient fashion: I am not angry with you, only, be gone!

---

18. Do you dread change? What can come without it? What can be pleasanter or more proper to universal nature? Can you heat your bath unless wood undergoes a change? Can you be fed unless a change is wrought upon your food? Can any useful thing be done without changes? Do you not see, then, that this change also which is working in you is even such as these, and alike necessary to the nature of the Universe?

---

19. Through the substance of the Universe, as through a torrent, all bodies are born. They are all of the same nature, and fellow workers with the whole, even as our several members are fellow workers with one another. How many a Chrysippus, how many a Socrates, how many an Epictetus hath the course of ages swallowed up! Let this thought be with you about every man, and upon all occasions.

20. For this alone I am concerned; that I do nothing that suits not the nature of man, nothing as man's nature would not have it, nothing that it wishes not yet.

---

21. The time is at hand when you shall forget all things, and when all shall forget you.

---

22. It is man's special business to love even those who err; and to this love you attain, if it is borne in upon you that even these sinners are your kin, and that they offend through ignorance and against their will. Remember also that in a little while both you and they must die: remember before all things that they have not harmed you, for they have not made your soul worse than it was before.

---

23. Presiding nature from the universal substance, as from wax, now forms a horse, now breaks it up again, making of its matter a tree, afterwards a man, and again something different. Each of these shapes subsists but for a little. Yet, there is

nothing dreadful for the chest in being taken to pieces, any more than there formerly was in being put together.

---

24. A wrathful look is completely against nature. When the countenance is often thus deformed, its beauty dies, in the end is quenched forever, and cannot be revived again. Seek to comprehend from this very fact that it is against reason. And if the sense of moral evil be gone as well, why should a man wish to remain alive?

---

25. In a little space Nature, the supreme and universal ruler, will change all things that you behold; out of their substance she will make other things, and others again out of the substance of these, so that the Universe may be ever new.

---

26. Whenever someone offends you, consider straightway how he has erred in his conceptions of good or evil. When you see where his error lies you will pity him, and be neither surprised

nor angry. Indeed, you yourself perhaps still wrongly count good the same things as he does, or things just like them. Your duty then is to forgive. And, if you cease from these false ideas of good and bad, you will find it the easier to grant indulgence to him who is still mistaken.

---

27. Dwell not on what you lack so much as on what you have already. Select the best of what you have, and consider how passionately you would have longed for it had it not been yours. Yet be watchful, lest by this joy in what you have you accustom yourself to value it too highly; so that, if it should fail, you would be distressed.

---

28. Retire within yourself. The reasoning power that rules you naturally finds contentment with itself in just dealing, and in the calm which such dealing brings.

---

29. Blot out imagination. Check the brutal impulses of the passions. Confine your energies to the present time. Observe clearly all that happens

either to yourself or to another. Divide and analyze all objects into cause and matter. Take thought for your last hour. Let another's sin remain where the guilt lies.

---

30. Apply your mind to what is said. Penetrate all happenings and the causes thereof.

---

31. Rejoice yourself with simplicity, modesty, and indifference to all things that lie between good and bad. Love mankind, and obey God. "All things," says someone, "go by law and order." But what if there be naught beyond the atoms? Even if that be so, suffice it to remember that all things, save very few, are swayed by law.

---

32. Concerning death: If the Universe be a concourse of atoms, death is a scattering of these; if it be an ordered unity, death is an extinction or a translation to another state.

33. Concerning pain: Pain which cannot be borne brings us deliverance. Pain that lasts musts needs be bearable. The mind can abstract itself from the body, and the soul takes no hurt. As to the parts which suffer by pain, let them, if they can, make their own protest.

---

34. Concerning glory: Consider the understanding of men, what they shun, and what they pursue. And reflect that, as heaps of sand are driven one upon another, and the later drifts bury and hide those that went before, so, too, in life the former ages are soon buried by the next.

---

35. This from Plato: "'To the man who has true grandeur of mind, and who contemplates all time and all being, can human life appear a great matter?' 'Impossible,' says the other. 'Can then such a one count death a thing of dread?' 'No, indeed.'"

36. It is a saying of Antisthenes, that it is the part of a king to do good and reap reproach.

---

37. It is a shameful thing that the countenance should obey the mind, should compose and order itself as the mind bids it, while the mind cannot compose and order itself as it wills.

---

38. *Vain is all anger at external things*
For they regard it nothing.

---

39. *Give joy to us and to the immortal Gods.*

---

40. *For life is, like the laden ear, cut down;*
And some must fall and some unreaped remain.

---

41. *Me and my children, if the Gods neglect,*
It is for some good reason.

42. *For I keep right and justice on my side.*

---

43. *Weep not with them, and still these throbs of woe.*

---

44. From Plato: "I would make him this just answer, 'You are mistaken, my friend, to think that a man of any worth should count the chances of living and dying. Should he not rather, in all he does, consider simply whether he is acting justly or unjustly, whether he is playing the part of a good man or a bad?'"

---

45. He says again: "In truth, Athenians, the matter stands thus: Wheresoever a man has chosen his stand, judging it the fittest for him, or wheresoever he is stationed by his commander, there, I think, he should stay at all hazards, making no account of death, or any other evil but dishonor."

---

46. Again: "Consider, my friend, whether the truly noble and the truly good be not something quite

apart from saving and being saved. The man who is a man indeed should not set his heart on living through a few more years of life, nor should he make that the end of his desire. Rather he should commit the matter to the will of God; assenting to the maxim which even women use, that 'no man can elude his destiny,' and studying in addition how he may spend the life that remains to him for the best."

---

47. Contemplate the courses of the stars, as one should do that revolves along with them. Consider also without ceasing the changes of elements, one into another. Speculations upon such things cleanse away the filth of this earthly life.

---

48. It is a good thought of Plato's, that when we discourse of men we should "look down, as from a high place," on all things earthly; on herds and armies; on husbandry and marriage; on partings, births, and deaths; on the tumults of the courts of justice; on the desert places of the earth; on the varied spectacle of savage nations; on feasting and lamentation; on traffic; on the medley of all things, and the order which emerges from their contrariety.

49. Consider the past, and the revolutions of so many Empires; and thence you may foresee what shall happen hereafter. It will be ever the same in all things; nor can events leave the rhythm in which they are now moving. Wherefore it is much the same to view human life for forty, as for a myriad of years. What more is there to see?

---

50. *To earth returns whatever sprang from earth,*
But what's of heavenly seed remounts to heaven.

52. He is a better wrestler than you, but not more public-spirited, more modest, or better prepared for the accidents of fate; not gentler toward the short-comings of his neighbors.

53. Wherever we can act conformably to the reason which is common to Gods and men, there we have nothing to dread. Where we can profit by prosperous activity which proceeds in agreement with the constitution of our nature, we need suspect no harm.

54. In all places, and at all times you may devoutly accept your present fortune, and deal in justice with your present company. You may take pains to understand all arising imaginations, that none may steal upon you before you comprehend them.

55. Pry not into the souls of others; but rather look straight to the goal whither nature is leading you; whither the nature of the Universe by

external events, and whither your own nature by the tendency of your own action. Each being must perform the part for which it was created. Now all other beings are created for the sake of those among them which have reason; as all lower things exist for the sake of things superior to them; and reasoning beings were created for one another. The leading principle in man's nature, then, is the social spirit; and the second is victory over the solicitations of the body. For it is proper to the workings of reason to set bounds to themselves, and never to be overpowered by the calls of sense or by the stirrings of passion, both of which are animal in their nature. The intellect claims to reign over these, and never to be subjected to them; and rightly, because it is equipped to command and use all the lower powers. The third element in the constitution of a reasoning being is caution against rashness and error. Let the soul go forth straight upon her way in the possession of these principles, and she stands seized of her full estate.

---

56. Consider yourself as dead, your life as finished and past. Live what yet remains according to Nature's laws, as an overplus granted to you beyond your hope.

57. Love that only which is your hap, which comes upon you as your part in Fate's great spinning. What, indeed, can fit you better?

---

58. Upon every accident keep in view those to whom the like has happened. They stormed at the event, wondered and complained. But now where are they? They are gone forever. Why should you act the like part? Leave these unnatural commotions to fickle men who change and are changed. Yourself take thought how you may make good use of such events. Good use for them there is; they will make matter for good actions. Let it be your sole effort and desire to gain your own approval in every action; and remember that the material objects of both that effort and of that desire are things indifferent.

---

59. Look inward. Within is the fountain of Good. Dig constantly and it will ever well forth.

---

60. Keep the body steady, without irregularity, whether in its motions or in its postures. For,

as the soul shews itself in the countenance by a wise and graceful air, it should require the same expressive power of the whole body. But all this must be practiced without affectation.

---

61. The art of Life is more like that of the wrestler than of the dancer; for the wrestler must always be ready on his guard, and stand firm against the sudden, unforeseen efforts of his adversary.

---

62. Consider constantly what manner of men they are whose approbation you desire, and what may be the character of their souls. Then you will neither accuse such as err unwillingly, nor need their commendation when you look into the springs of their opinions and their desires.

---

63. "Every soul," says Plato, "parts unwillingly with truth." You may say the same of justice, temperance, good-nature, and every virtue. It is most necessary to keep this ever in mind; for, if you do, you will be kindlier towards all men.

64. In all pain keep in mind that there is no baseness in it, that it cannot harm the soul which guides you, nor destroy that soul as a reasoning or as a social force. In most pain you may find help in the saying of Epicurus, that "pain is neither unbearable nor everlasting, if you bear in mind its narrow limits, and allow no additions from your imagination." Remember also that we are fretted, though we see it not, by many things which are of the same nature as pain, things such as drowsiness, excessive heat, want of appetite. When any of these things annoy you, say to yourself that you are giving in to pain.

---

65. Look to it that you feel not towards the most inhuman of mankind, as they feel towards their fellows.

---

66. Whence do we conclude that Telauges had not a brighter genius than Socrates? 'Tis not enough that Socrates died more gloriously or argued more acutely with the sophists; or that he kept watch more patiently through a frosty night; or because, when ordered to arrest the innocent

Salaminian, he judged it more noble to disobey; or because of any stately airs and graces he assumed in public, in which we may very justly refuse to believe. But, assuming all this true, when we consider Socrates, we must ask what manner of soul he had. Could he find contentment in acting with justice towards men, and with piety towards the Gods, neither vainly provoked by the vices of others, nor servilely flattering them in their ignorance; counting nothing strange that the Ruler of the Universe appointed, not sinking under anything as intolerable, and never yielding up his soul in surrender to the passions of the flesh.

---

67. Nature has not so blended the soul with the body that it cannot fix its own bounds, and execute its own office by itself. It is very possible to be a God among men, and yet be recognized by none. Remember that always, and this as well, that the happiness of life lies in very few things. And though you despair of becoming great in Logic or in Science, you need not despair of becoming a free man, full of modesty and unselfishness, and of obedience unto God.

68. It is in your power to live superior to all violence, and in the greatest calm of mind, were all men to rail against you as they pleased; and though wild beasts were to tear asunder the wretched members of this fleshly mass which has grown with your growth. What is to hinder the soul amid all this from preserving itself in all tranquility, in just judgments about surrounding things, and in ready use of whatever is cast in its way? Judgment may say to accident: "Your real nature is this or that, though you appear otherwise in the eyes of men." Use may say to circumstance: "I was looking for you. To me all that is present is ever matter for rational and social virtue, in sum, for that art which is proper both to man and God. All that befalls is fit and familiar for the purposes of God or man. Nothing is either new or intractable, but everything is well known and fit to work upon."

---

69. It is the perfection of morals to spend each day as if it were the last of life, without excitement, without sloth, and without hypocrisy.

THE EIGHTH BOOK

1. For repressing vain glory, it serves to remember that it is no longer in your power to make your whole life, even from your youth onwards, a life worthy of a philosopher. It is known to many, and you yourself know also, how far you are from wisdom. Confusion is upon you, and it now can be no easy matter for you to gain the reputation of a philosopher. The conditions of your life are against it. Now therefore, as you see how the matter truly lies, put from you all thoughts of reputation among men; and let it suffice you to live so long as your nature wills, though that be but the scanty remnant of a life. Study, therefore, the will of your nature, and be solicitous about nothing else. You have made many efforts and wandered much, but you have nowhere found happiness; not in syllogisms, not in riches, not in fame or pleasure, not in anything. Where, then,

is it? In acting that part which human nature requires. How can you act that part? By holding principles as the source of your desires and actions. What principles? The principles of good and evil: That nothing is good for a man which does not make him just, temperate, courageous, and free; and that nothing can be evil which tends not to make him the contrary of all these.

---

2. Upon every action ask yourself, what is the effect of this for me? Shall I never repent of it? I shall presently be dead, and all these things gone. What more should I desire if my present action is becoming to an intelligent and a social being, subject to the same law with Gods?

---

3. Alexander, Caesar, Pompey, what were they compared with Diogenes, Heraclitus, Socrates? These knew the nature of things, their causes and their matter, and the minds within them were at one. As to the former, how many things they schemed for, and to how many were they enslaved!

4. Men will go their ways none the less, though you burst in protest.

---

5. Before all things, be not perturbed. Everything comes to pass as directed by universal Nature, and in a little time you will be departed and gone, like Hadrianus and Augustus. Then, scan closely the nature of what has befallen, remembering that it is your duty to be a good man. Do unflinchingly whatever man's nature requires, and speak as seems most just, yet in kindliness, modesty, and sincerity.

---

6. It is Nature's work to transfer what is now here into another place, to change things, to carry them hence, and set them elsewhere. All is change, yet is there no need to fear innovation, for all obey the laws of custom, and in equal measure all things are apportioned.

---

7. For every nature it is sufficient that it goes on its way, and prospers. The rational nature prospers while it assents to no false or uncertain opinion,

while it directs its impulses to unselfish ends alone, while it aims its desires and aversions only at the things within its power, and while it welcomes with contentment all that universal Nature ordains. The nature of each of us is part of universal Nature, as the leaf is part of the tree; the leaf, indeed, is part of an insensible and unreasoning system which can be obstructed in its workings; but human nature is part of that universal system which cannot be impeded, and which is intelligent and just. Hence is meted out, suitably to all, our proper portions of time, of matter, of active principle, of powers, and of events. Yet look not to find that each several thing corresponds exactly with any other. Consider rather the whole nature and circumstances of the one, and compare them with the whole of the other.

---

8. You lack leisure for reading; but leisure to repress all insolence you do not lack. You have leisure to keep yourself superior to pleasure and pain and vain glory, to restrain all anger against the ungrateful, nay, even to lavish loving care upon them.

9. Let no man any more hear you railing on the life of the court; nay, revile it not to your own hearing.

---

10. Repentance is a self-reproving, because we have neglected something useful. Whatever is good must be useful in some sort, and worthy of the care of a good and honorable man. Now, such a man could never repent of neglecting some opportunity of pleasure. Pleasure, then, is neither useful nor good.

---

11. Of each thing ask: What is this in itself and by its constitution? What is its substance or matter? What is its cause? What is its business in the Universe? How long shall it endure?

---

12. When you are reluctant to be roused from sleep, remember that it accords with your constitution and with human nature to perform social actions. Sleep is common to us with the brutes. Now, whatever accords with the nature of each species must be most proper, most fitting, and most delightful to it.

13. Constantly, and, if possible, on every occasion, apply to your imaginations the methods of Physics, Ethics, and Dialectic.

---

14. Whomsoever you meet, say straightway to yourself: What are this man's principles of good and evil? For if he holds this or that doctrine concerning pleasure and pain, and the causes thereof, concerning glory and infamy, death and life, it will seem to me neither strange nor wondrous that this or that should be his conduct. I shall bear in mind that he has no choice but to act so.

---

15. Remember that, as 'tis folly to be surprised that a fig tree bears figs, so is it equal folly to be surprised that the Universe produces those things of which it was ever fruitful. It is folly in a physician to be surprised that a man has fallen into a fever; or in a pilot that the wind has turned against him.

16. Remember that to change your course, and to follow any man who can set you right is no compromise of your freedom. The act is your own, performed on your own impulse and judgment, and according to your own understanding.

---

17. If the doing of this be in your own power, why do it thus? If it be in another's, whom do you accuse? The atoms or the Gods? To accuse either is a piece of madness. Therefore accuse no one. Set right, if you can, the cause of error; if you cannot, correct the result at least. If even that be impossible, what purpose can your accusations serve? Nothing should be done without a purpose.

---

18. That which dies falls not out of the Universe. If then it stays here, here too it suffers a change, and is resolved into those elements of which the world, and you too, consist. These also are changed, and murmur not.

19. The horse, the vine—all things are formed for some purpose. Where is the wonder? Even the sun says, "I was formed for a certain work;" and similarly the other Gods. For what end are you formed? For pleasure? Look if your soul can endure this thought.

---

20. Nature has an aim in all things, in the end and surcease of them no less than in their beginning and continuance. It is even as a man casting a ball. Where, then, is the good for the ball in its rising; where the harm in dropping; where even is the harm when it has fallen down? Where is the bubble's good while it holds together, where is the evil when it is broken? So, it is with the lamp which now burns and anon goes out.

---

21. Turn out the inner side of this body, and view it as it is. What shall it become when it grows old, or sickly, or decayed? The praiser and the praised, the rememberer and the remembered are of short continuance, and that in a mere corner of this narrow region, where, narrow though it

be, men cannot live in concord, no, not even with themselves. And yet the whole world is but a point.

---

22. Attend well to what is before you, whether it be a principle, an act, or a word. This your suffering is well merited, for you would rather become good tomorrow than be good today.

---

23. Am I doing aught? Let me do it in a spirit of service to mankind. Does aught befall me? I accept it and refer it to the Gods, the universal source from which come all things in the chain of consequence.

---

24. The accompaniments of bathing: oil, sweat, filth, foul water—how nauseous are they all! Even so is every part of life, and everything that meets us.

25. Lucilla buried Verus, and soon followed him to the grave. Secunda saw the death of Maximus, and soon herself died. Epitynchanus buried Diotimus, and then Epitynchanus was buried. Antoninus mourned Faustina, and thereafter Antoninus was mourned. Celer buried Hadrian, and then Celer was buried. All go the same way. The cunning men who foretold the fates of others, or who swelled with pride—where are they now? Where are these keen wits, Charax, and Demetrius the Platonist, and Eudaemon, and their like? All were for a day, and are long dead and gone; some scarce remembered even for a little after death; some turned to fables; some faded even from the memory of tales. Wherefore remember this: either the poor mixture which is you, must be dispersed, or the faint breath of life must be quenched, or removed and brought into another place.

---

26. The joy of man is to do his proper business. And his proper business is to be kindly to his fellows, to rise above the stirrings of sense, to be critical of every plausible imagination, and to contemplate universal Nature and all her consequences.

27. We have all of us three relations: the first to the manifold occasions of our state; the second to the supreme divine cause from which proceed all things unto all men; the third to those with whom we live.

---

28. Pain is either an evil to the body; and then let the body so declare it; or an evil to the soul. But the soul can maintain her own serenity and calm; and refuse to conceive pain as an evil. All judgment, intention, desire and aversion are within the soul, to which no evil can ascend.

---

29. Blot out false imaginations, and say often to yourself: It is now in my power to preserve my soul free from all wickedness, all lust, all confusion or disturbance. And then, as I truly discern the nature of things, I can use them all in due proportion. Be ever mindful of this power which Nature has given you.

30. Speak, whether in the Senate or elsewhere, with dignity rather than elegance; and let your words ever be sound and virtuous.

---

31. The court of Augustus, his wife, his daughter, his descendants and his ancestors; his sister, and Agrippa; his kinsmen, familiars and friends; Areius and Maecenas; his physicians and his flamens—death has them all. Think next of the death of a whole house, such as Pompey's, and of what we meet sometimes inscribed on tombs: *He was the last of his race. Last of all, consider the solicitude of the ancestors of such men to leave a succession of their own posterity. Yet, at the end, one must come the last, and with him dies all that house.*

---

32. Order your life in its single acts, so that if each, as far as may be, attains its end, it will suffice. In this no one can hinder you. "But," you say, "may not something external withstand me? Nothing can keep you from justice, temperance, and wisdom. Yet, perhaps some other activity of mine may be obstructed." True, but by yielding to this impediment, and by turning with calmness to

that which is in your power, you may happen on another course of action equally suited to the ordered life of which we are speaking.

33. Receive the gifts of fortune without pride; and part with them without reluctance.

34. You have seen a hand, a foot, or a head, cut off from the rest of the body, and lying dead at a distance from it. Even such as these does he make himself, so far as he can, who repines at what befalls, who severs himself from his fellow men, or who does any selfish deed. Are you cast forth from the natural unity? Nature made you to be a part of the whole, but you have cut yourself off from it. Yet here there is the glorious provision that you may reunite yourself if you will. In no other case has God granted the privilege of reunion to a separated or severed part. Yet behold the goodness and bounty with which God hath honored mankind. He first puts it in their power not to be severed from this unity; and then, even when they are thus severed, he suffers them to return once more, to take their places as parts of the whole, and to grow one with it again.

reason. "I am not reason," you say. So be it; then let not reason pain itself, but leave any part of you which suffers to its own opinions of the pain.

41. Obstruction of any sense is an evil for the animal nature; so is the obstruction of any of its impulses. There are other kinds of obstruction which are evil for the nature of plants. For the rational nature in like manner, therefore, obstruction of the understanding is evil. Apply all this to yourself. Do pain and pleasure affect you? Let the senses look to it. Does anything hinder your designs? If you have designed without the proper reservations, that in itself is an evil for you as a reasoning being. If you designed under the general reservation, you are neither hurt nor hindered. No man can hinder the proper work of the mind. Nor fire, nor sword, nor tyrant, nor calumny can reach it, nor any other thing, when it is become even as a sphere, complete and perfect within itself.

42. I have no right to vex myself who never yet willingly vexed anyone.

43. Each man has his own pleasure. Mine lies in having my ruling part sound; without aversion to any man, or to any hap that may befall mankind. Yet let me look on all things with kindly eyes. Let me accept and use them all according to their worth.

---

44. See that you secure the benefit of the present time. They who pursue a fame which is to live after them reflect not that posterity will be men even as are those who vex them now, and that they too will be mortal. And afterwards, what shall signify to you the clatter of their voices, or the opinions they shall entertain about you?

---

45. Take me up and cast me where you will; I shall have my own divinity within me serene, that is, satisfied while its every state and action is according to the law of its proper constitution.

Is any event of such account that my soul should suffer for it or be the worse; that my soul should become abject and prostrate as a mean suppliant, or should be affrighted? Shall you find anything that is worth all this?

46. Nothing can befall a man which is not human fortune. Nothing can happen to an ox, to a vine, or to a stone which is not the natural destiny of their species. If, then, that alone can befall anything which is usual and natural, what cause is there for indignation? Universal Nature hath brought nothing upon you which you cannot bear.

---

47. When you are grieved about anything external it is not the thing itself which afflicts you, but your judgment about it. This judgment it is in your power to efface. If you are grieved about anything in your own disposition, who can prevent you from correcting your principles of life? If you are grieved because you do not set about some work which seems to you sound and virtuous, go about it effectually rather than grieve that it is undone. "But some superior force withstands." Then grieve not, for the fault of the omission lies not in you. "But life is not worth living with this undone." Quit life then, in the same kindly spirit as though you had done it, and with goodwill even to those who withstand you.

48. Remember that the governing part becomes invincible when, collected into itself, it is satisfied in refusing to do what it would not, even when its resistance is unreasonable. What then will it be when, after due deliberation it has fixed its judgment according to reason? The soul, thus free from passions, is a strong fort; nor can a man find any stronger to which he can fly and become henceforth invincible. The man who has not discerned this is ignorant. He who has discerned and flies not thither is miserable.

---

49. Pronounce no more to yourself than what appearances directly declare. It is told you that so-and-so has spoken ill of you. This alone is told you, and not that you are hurt by it. I see my child is sick; this only I see. I do not see that he is in danger. Dwell thus upon first appearances; add nothing to them from within, and no harm befalls you: or rather add the recognition that all is part of the world's lot.

---

50. Is the gourd bitter? Put it from you. Are there thorns in the way? Walk aside. That is enough. Do not add, "Why were such things brought

into the world?" The naturalist would laugh at you, just as would a carpenter or a shoemaker, if you began fault-finding because you saw shavings and parings from their work strewn about the workshop. These craftsmen have places where they can throw away this rubbish, but universal Nature has no such place outside her sphere. Yet the wonder of her art is that, having confined herself within certain bounds, she transforms into herself all things within her scope which seem to be corrupting, or waxing old and useless; and out of them she makes other new forms; so that she neither needs matter from without nor a place where to cast out her refuse. She is satisfied with her own space, her own material, and her own art.

---

51. Be not languid in action, nor confused in conversation, nor vague in your opinions. Let there be no sudden contractions or forth-sallyings of your soul. In your life be not over hurried.

Men slay you, cut you to pieces, pursue you with curses. What has this to do with your soul remaining pure, prudent, temperate, and just? What if someone, standing by a clear sweet fountain, should reproach it? It would not cease to send forth its refreshing waters. Should he throw into it mud or dung, it will speedily scatter them and wash them away, and be in nowise stained thereby. How then shall you get this perpetual living fount within you? If you reserve yourself unto liberty every hour you live, in a spirit of calmness, simplicity, and modesty.

---

52. He who knows not what the Universe is knows not what is his place therein. He who knows not for what end it was created, knows not himself and knows not the world. He who is deficient in either of these parts of knowledge cannot even say for what end he himself was created. What sort of man then does he appear to you who pursues the applause or dreads the anger of those who know neither where nor what they are?

---

53. Do you wish to be praised by a man who curses himself thrice within an hour? Can you desire to please one who is not pleased with himself? Can he be pleased with himself who repents of almost everything he does?

54. No longer be content to breathe in harmony with the air which surrounds you; but set about feeling in sympathy with the intelligence which embraces all things. For the power of that intelligence is no less diffused, and no less pervasive for all who can draw it in, than is the virtue of the air for him who can breathe it.

---

55. There is no universal wickedness to hurt the world; and the particular wickedness of any individual hurts not another. It hurts himself alone, and even he has this gracious privilege that, as soon as he desires it, he may be free from it altogether.

---

56. To my will the will of another is as indifferent as his poor breath and flesh. And how much soever we were formed for the sake of each other, yet the governing part of each of us has its own proper power; otherwise, the vice of another might become my own misery. God thought fit that this should not be; lest it should be in another's power to make me unhappy.

57. The sun seems to us diffused everywhere, pervasive of all things, yet never exhausted. This diffusion is a sort of extension, and hence the Greek word for rays is thought to be derived. You may observe the nature of a ray if you see it entering through some small hole into a darkened chamber. Its direction is straight; and it is reflected around when it falls upon any solid body, which shuts it off from the air beyond. There it stands and does not slip or fall. Now, such should be the flow and diffusion of the understanding; never exhausted, always extending; not violently or furiously dashing against the obstacles that meet it, nor falling aside, but resting there and illuminating whatever will receive it. That which will not transmit the light does but deprive itself of radiance.

---

58. He who dreads death dreads either the extinction of all sense or the experience of a new one. If all sense be extinguished, there can be no sense of evil. If a different sort of sense be acquired you become a different creature, and do not cease to live.

59. Men were created the one for the other. Teach them better then, or bear with them.

---

60. Mind moves in one way, and an arrow in another. The mind, when cautiously proceeding, or when casting round in deliberation about what to pursue, is nevertheless carried onward straight toward its proper mark.

---

61. Penetrate into the governing part of others; and also allow others to enter into your own.

THE NINTH BOOK

1. He who does injustice commits impiety. For since universal Nature has formed the rational animals for one another; each to be useful to the other according to his merit, and never hurtful; he who transgresses this her will is clearly guilty of impiety against the most ancient and venerable of the Gods.

He who lies sins against the same divinity. For the nature of the whole is the nature of all things which exist; and things which exist are akin to all that has come to be. Nature, indeed, is called truth, and is the first cause of all truths. He, then, that lies willingly is guilty of impiety, in so far as by deceiving he works injury: and he also who lies unwillingly, in so far as he is out of tune with universal Nature, and in so far as he works disorder in the Universe by fighting against its design. He is at war with Nature who sets himself against the truth. He has neglected the means with which Nature furnished him, and cannot now distinguish false from true.

He, too, who pursues pleasure as good, and shuns pain as evil, is guilty of impiety. Such a one must needs frequently blame the common nature for unseemly awards of fortune to bad and to good men. For the bad often enjoy pleasures and possess the means to attain them, and the good often meet with pain and with what causes pain. Again, he who dreads pain must sometimes dread a thing which will make part of the world order, and this is impious. And he who pursues pleasure will not abstain from injustice, and this is clear impiety. In those things to which the common nature is indifferent (for she had not made both, were she not indifferent to either), he who would follow Nature ought, in this also, to be of like mind with her, and shew the like indifference. And whoever is not indifferent to pain and pleasure, life and death, glory and ignominy, all of which universal Nature uses indifferently, is clearly impious. By Nature using them indifferently, I mean that they befall indifferently all beings which exist, and ensue upon others in the great chain of consequence which began in the primal impulse of Providence. Providence, in pursuance of this impulse, and starting from a definite beginning, set about this fair structure of the universe when she had conceived the plan of all that was to be, and appointed the distinct powers which were to produce the several substances, changes, and successions.

---

2. It were the more desirable lot to depart from among men, unacquainted with falsehood, hypocrisy, luxury, or vanity. The next choice is to expire when cloyed with these vices. Have you then chosen rather to abide in evil; or has experience not yet persuaded you to fly from amidst the plague? For a corruption of the mind is far more a plague than any pestilential distemper or change in the surrounding air we breathe. The one is pestilence to animals as animals: but the other to men as men.

---

3. Despise not death; but receive it well content, as one of the things which Nature wills. For even as it is to be young, to be old, to grow up, to be full grown; even as it is to breed teeth, and beard, and to grow grey, to beget, to go with child, to be delivered; and to undergo all the effects of nature which life's seasons bring; such is it also to be dissolved in death. It becomes not

therefore a man of wisdom to be careless, or impatient, or ostentatiously contemptuous about death; he should rather await its coming as one of the operations of nature. Even as now you await the season when the child of your wife's body shall issue into the light, await the hour when your soul shall fall out of these its teguments. If you wish for the common sort of comfort, here is a thought which goes to the heart. You will be completely resigned to death if you consider the things you are about to leave, and the morals of that confused crowd from which your soul is to be disengaged. It is far from right to be offended with them. It is even your duty to have a tender care for them, and to bear with them mildly. Yet remember that the parting, when it comes, will not be with men who think as you think. For the only thing which, if it might be, could hold you back and detain you in life, would be to live with those who had reached the same principles of life as you. But, as it is, you, seeing how great is the fatigue and toil arising from the jarring courses of those who live together, may cry: "Haste, death! Lest I, too, should forget myself."

4. The sinner sins against himself. The wrongdoer wrongs himself by making himself evil.

---

5. Men are often unjust by omissions as well as by actions.

---

6. Be satisfied with your present opinion, if certain; with your present course of action, if social; with your present mood, if well pleased with all that comes upon you from without.

---

7. Wipe out impression; stay impulse; quench desire; and keep the governing part master of itself.

---

8. The soul distributed among the irrational animals is one. Rational beings, on the other hand, partake of one reasoning intelligence. Even so, there is one earth to all things earthy; and, for all of us who are endowed with sight and breath, there is one light by which to see, one air to breathe.

9. All things that share a common quality are strongly drawn to that which is of their own kind. The earthy tends towards the earth; fluids flow together, aerial bodies likewise; and naught but force prevents their confluence. Fire rises upward on account of the elemental fire; and it is so ready to join in kindling with all the fire that is here that any matter pretty dry is easily set on fire, because that which hinders its kindling is the weaker element in its composition. Thus also, then, whatever partakes of the common intellectual nature hastens in like manner, or even more markedly, towards that which is akin to it. For the more it excels other natures, the stronger is its tendency to mix with and adhere to its kind. Accordingly, among irrational creatures we find swarms of bees, herds of cattle, nurture of the young, and love, of a sort. For even in animals there is a soul; and in the more noble natures a mutual attraction is found to be at work, such as does not exist in plants, or stones, or wood. Among the rational animals, again, there are societies and friendships, families and assemblies; and, in war, treaties and truces. Among beings still more excellent, there subsists, though they be placed far asunder, a certain kind of union, as among the stars. Thus, ascent in the scale can produce a sympathy even in things that are

widely distant. But mark what happens among us. It is only intellectual beings who forget the social concern for one another, and the mutual tendency to union. Here alone the social confluence is not seen. Yet are they environed and held by it, though they strive to escape; and nature always prevails. Observe and you will see my meaning: for sooner may one find some earthy thing which joins with nothing earthy, than a man severed and separate from all men.

---

10. Man, God, and the Universe, all bear fruit; and each in their own season. Custom indeed has appropriated the expression to vines and the like; but that is nothing. Reason has its fruit both for all men and for itself, and produces just such other things as reason itself is.

---

11. If you can, teach men better. If not, remember that the virtue of charity was given you to be used in such a case. Nay, the Gods are patient with them, and even aid them in their pursuit of some things such as health, wealth, and glory, so gracious are they! You may be so too. Who hinders you?

12. Bear toil and pain, not as if wretched under it, nor as courting pity or admiration. Wish for one thing only; always to act or to refrain as social wisdom requires.

---

13. Today I have escaped from all trouble; or rather I have cast out all trouble from me. For it was not without but within, in my own opinions.

---

14. All things are, in our experience, common; in their continuance but for a day; and in their matter sordid. All things now are as they were in the times of those we have buried.

---

15. Things stand without, by themselves, neither knowing or declaring aught to us concerning themselves. What is it then that pronounces upon them? The ruling part.

16. It is not in passive feeling, but in action, that the good and evil of the rational animal formed for society consists. Similarly, his virtue or his vice lies not in feeling but in action.

---

17. To the stone thrown up it is no evil to fall; no good to rise.

---

18. Penetrate the souls of men, and you will see what judges you fear, and how they sit in judgment on themselves.

---

19. All things are in change. You yourself are under continual transmutation, and, in some sort, corruption. So is the whole universe.

---

20. Another's sin you must leave with himself.

21. The ceasing of any action, the extinction of any keen desire, or of any opinion, is as it were a death to them. This is no evil. Think again of the ages of your life; childhood, youth, manhood, old age. Each change of these was a death. Is there anything to dread here? Think now of your life as it was, first under your grandfather, then under your mother, then under your father; and, as you find there many other alterations, changes, and endings, ask yourself: Is there anything to dread here? Thus, neither is there anything to dread in the cessation, ending, and change of your whole life.

---

22. Make swift appeal to your own ruling part, to that of the Universe, and to his who has offended you. To your own, that you may make it a mind disposed to justice; to that of the Universe, that you may remember of what you are a part; and to his, that you may know whether he has acted in ignorance or by design, and that you may also reflect that he is your kinsman.

---

23. You yourself are a part of a social system necessary to complete the whole. Accordingly,

let your every action be a similar part of the social life. And if any action has not its reference, either immediate or distant, to the common good as its end, this action disorders your life and frustrates its unity. It is sedition like that of the man who, in a commonwealth, does all in his power to sever himself from the general harmony and concord.

---

24. Children's quarrels! Child's play! Poor spirits carrying about dead corpses! Such is our life. The "Masque of the Dead" is intelligible by comparison.

---

25. Go to the quality of the cause; abstract it from the material, and contemplate it by itself. Determine then the time: how long, at furthest, this thing, of this peculiar quality, can naturally subsist.

---

26. You have endured innumerable sufferings by not being satisfied with your own ruling part when it does the things which it was formed to do. Enough then of that.

27. When another reproaches or hates you, or utters anything to that purpose; go to his soul; enter in there; and look what manner of man he is. You will see that you need not trouble yourself to make him think well or ill of you. Yet you should be kindly towards such men, for they are by nature your friends: and the Gods, too, aid them in all ways; by dreams, by oracles, and even in the things about which they are most eager.

---

28. The course of things in the world is ever the same; a continual rotation; up and down, from age to age. Either the Universal Mind exerts itself in every particular event, in which case you must accept what comes immediately from it: or it has exerted itself once and for all, and, as a result, all things go on forever, in a necessary chain of consequence: or again atoms and indivisible particles are the origin of all things. In fine, if there be a God, all is well; and if there be only chance, you at least need not act by chance.

The earth will presently cover us all; and then this earth will itself be changed into other forms, and these again into others, and so on without end. And, if any one considers how swiftly those changes and transmutations roll on, like one wave upon another, he will despise all things mortal.

29. The universal cause is like a winter torrent. It sweeps all along with it. How very little worth are those poor creatures who pretend to understand affairs of state, and imagine they unite in themselves the statesman and the philosopher! The frothy fools! Do you, O man! that which Nature now requires of you. Set about it if you have the means; and look not around you to see if any be taking notice, neither hope to realize Plato's Republic. Be satisfied if the smallest thing go well. Consider even such an event as no small matter. For who can change the opinions of men? And without change of opinion what is their state but a slavery, under which they groan, while they pretend to obey? Come now; speak of Alexander, Philip, and Demetrius of Phalerum. They know best whether they understood what the common nature required of them, and whether they trained themselves accordingly. But, if they designed only to play the tragic hero, no one has condemned me to do the like. The work of philosophy is simple and modest. Lead me not astray in pursuit of a vainglorious stateliness.

30. Look down, as from some eminence, upon the innumerable herds, the countless solemn festivals, the voyaging of every sort, in tempests and in calms; the different states of those who come into life, enter upon life's associations, and leave it in the end. Consider, too, the life which others have lived formerly, the life they will live after you, and the life that barbarous peoples are now living. How many of these know not even your name; how many will quickly forget it; how many are there who perhaps praise you now, but will shortly blame you. Reflect, then, that neither is surviving fame a thing of value; nor present glory; nor anything at all.

31. Let nothing due to a cause outside yourself disturb your calm. In the workings of the active principle within you, let there be justice: that is a bent of will and a course of action which have social good as their one end, and so are suited to your nature.

32. You can suppress many of the superfluous troubles which beset you, for they lie wholly in your own opinion. By this you will give ample

room and ease to your life. You may compass this end by comprehending the whole Universe in your judgment; by contemplating eternity; and by reflecting on the swift changes of individual things, thinking how short is the time from their birth to their dissolution, how immense the space of ages before that birth, how equally infinite the eternity which shall succeed that dissolution.

---

33. All things that you see will quickly perish; and those who behold them perishing are very soon themselves to die. And he who dies oldest will be in like case with him who dies before his time.

---

34. What manner of souls have these men? What is the end of their striving; and on what accounts do they love and honor? Imagine their souls naked before you. When they fancy that their censures hurt, or their praises profit us, how great is their self-conceit!

35. Loss is naught but change; in change is the joy of universal Nature, and by her all things are ordered well. From the beginning of ages, they have been shaped alike, and to all eternity they will be the same. How then can you say that all things have been, and ever will be evil; that among so many Gods there has been found no power to rectify; but that the Universe is condemned to endure the burden of never-ending ill?

---

36. How corrupt is the material substance of everything, water, dust, bones, and foulness! Again; marble is but the concrete humor of the earth, gold and silver its heavy dregs. Our garments are but hair, the purple dye blood. All else is of a like nature. Breath, too, is just the same, ever changing from this to that.

---

37. Enough of this wretched life: enough of repining and apish trifling. Why are you disturbed? Are any of these troubles new? What excites you so? Is it the cause?

Then view it well. Is it the matter? View it also well. Besides these there is nothing. Wherefore at last act with more simplicity and goodness towards the Gods. Whether you look on this spectacle for a hundred years or for three it is the same.

---

38. If he has done wrong, the evil is with him: and perhaps, too, he has not done wrong.

---

39. Either all things proceed from one source of intelligence and come together in one body, in which case the part must not complain of what comes about for the benefit of the whole; or all is atoms, and there is nothing else but confused mixture and dissipation. Why then are you disturbed? Say to your soul: "You are dead: you are rotten: you have turned beast, joined the herd, and feed along with them."

---

40. Either the Gods have power or they have none. If they have no power, why do you pray? If they have power, why do you not choose to pray to them for power neither to fear, nor to desire, nor to be grieved over any of these external things, rather than for their presence or their absence?

Surely, if the Gods can aid man at all, they can aid him in this. But perhaps you will say, "the Gods have put this in my own power." Then is it not better to use that which is in your own power and preserve your liberty, than to set your heart on what is beyond your power and become an abject slave? And who has told you that the Gods aid us not in these things also which are in our power? Begin to pray about them and you will see. One man prays: "May I possess that woman!" Do you pray: "May I have no wish to possess her!" Another prays: "May I be delivered from so and so!" Pray you: "May I not need to be delivered from him!" A third cries: "May I not lose my child!" Let your prayer be: "May I not fear to lose him!" In fine, turn your prayers this way, and observe what comes of it.

---

41. Epicurus says: "In my sickness, my conversations were not about the diseases of this poor body; nor did I speak of any such things to those who came to me. I continued to discourse as before on the principles of natural Philosophy, and was chiefly intent on the problem of how the mind, though it partakes in the violent commotions of the flesh, might remain undisturbed and keep guard on its own proper excellence. I permitted not the

physicians," he continues, "to magnify their office, and vaunt themselves as if they were doing-something of great moment, but my life continued pleasant and happy." What he did then, in sickness, do you also if ye fall ill, or suffer any other misfortune. Never to depart from your philosophy whatever befalls you, never to join in the folly of the vulgar and the ignorant, is a maxim common to all the schools. Give your mind only to the business now in hand and to the means whereby it is to be accomplished.

---

42. When you are offended by the shamelessness of any man, straightway ask yourself: Can the world exist without shameless men? It cannot. Therefore, do not demand what is impossible. Your enemy also is one of these shameless people who must needs be in the universe. Have the same question also at hand when you are shocked at craft, or perfidy, or any other sin. For while you remember that it is impossible that the class should not exist, you will be more charitable to each particular individual. It is useful also to have this reflection ready: What virtue has nature given to man wherewith to combat this fault? Against unreason she has given meekness as an antidote; against another

weakness another power. You are also at full liberty to set right one who has wandered; now every wrongdoer is missing his proper aim and has gone astray. And then, in what are you injured? You will find that none of those at whom you are exasperated have done anything whereby your intellectual part was like to be the worse. Now anything which can really harm or hurt you has its subsistence there, and there alone. And wherein is it strange or evil that the man untaught acts after his kind? Look if you ought not rather to blame yourself for not having laid your account with his being guilty of such faults. Your reason gave you the means to conclude that it was probable that he would do this wrong; you forgot, and yet wonder that he has done it. But above all, when you are blaming any one for faithlessness or ingratitude, turn to yourself. The fault lies manifestly with you, if you trusted that a man of such a disposition could keep faith; or if, when you granted the favor, you did not grant it without ulterior views, and on the principle that the complete and immediate reward of your action lay in the doing of it. What would you more, when you have done a man a kindness? Is it not enough for you that you have acted in this according to your nature? Do you ask a reward for it? It is as if the eye were to ask a reward for seeing, or the feet for walking. For just as these parts are formed for a certain purpose, which when they fulfil according to their proper structure, they attain their proper end; so, man, formed by nature to do kindness to his fellows, whenever he acts kindly, or in any other way works for the common good, has fulfilled the purpose of his creation, and has possession of what is his own

THE TENTH BOOK

1. Will you ever, O my soul, be good and single, and one, and naked, more open to view than the body which surrounds you? Will you ever taste of the loving and satisfied temper? Will you ever be full and without wants, setting your heart on nothing, animate or inanimate, for the enjoyment of pleasure; not desiring time for longer enjoyment; nor place, nor country, nor fine climate, nor congenial company? Will you be satisfied with your present state, and well pleased with every present circumstance? Will you persuade yourself that all things are yours; that all is well with you; that all comes to you from the Gods; and that what is best for you is what they are pleased to give, now and henceforth, for the preservation of that perfected being, which is good, just, and beautiful; which generates,

themselves? Will you never be able to live a fellow citizen with Gods and men, approving them and by them approved?

---

2. In so far as you are governed by nature only, observe carefully what nature demands; then do that freely, if thereby your nature as a living being be not made worse. Next you must consider what the nature of a living being demands, and allow yourself everything of this kind by which your nature as a rational being is not made worse. Now it is plain that what is rational is also social. Therefore, follow these rules and trouble no further.

---

3. Whatever happens, Nature has either formed you able to bear it or unable. If able, then bear it as Nature has made you able, and fret not. If unable, yet do not fret, for when the trial has consumed you it too will pass away. Remember, however, that Nature has made you able to bear whatever it is in the power of your own opinion to make endurable or tolerable, if only you conceive it profitable or fit to be borne.

4. If a man is going wrong, instruct him kindly, and shew him his mistake. If you are unable to do this, blame yourself or none.

---

5. Whatever happens to you was prearranged for you from all eternity; and the concatenation of causes had from eternity interwoven your existence with this contingency.

---

6. Whether all be atoms, or there be a universal Law of Nature, let it be laid down first that I am a part of the whole which is governed by Nature; secondly, that I am associated with other parts like myself. Mindful of this, since I am a part, I shall not be dissatisfied with anything appointed me by the whole. For nothing is hurtful to the part which is profitable to the whole, since the whole contains nothing unprofitable to itself. All natural systems have this law in common, and the system of the Universe has another law besides; namely that it cannot be forced by any external cause to produce anything hurtful to itself. If therefore I remember that I am part of such a whole, I shall be satisfied with all that

flows therefrom. And, inasmuch as I am associated with parts like myself, I will do nothing unsocial; but rather draw to my kind, turn my every endeavor to the public good, and shun the contrary. In such a course my life must needs run well, just as you would hold that the life of a citizen runs well when he passes on from one public-spirited action to another, and throws himself heartily into every task appointed him by the State.

---

7. The parts of the whole, I mean the parts which are contained in the Universe, must necessarily perish; "perish," let us say, meaning change. Now, if it be a necessary evil for the parts to perish, it could not be well for the whole that its parts should tend to change and be constructed to perish in various ways. Did Nature then set out to injure her own constituent parts, making them so that they are liable to evil and of necessity fall into it; or did it escape her notice that this comes to pass? Both suppositions are incredible. And if, dropping the notion of Nature, one were merely to put it that things are constituted so, then how ridiculous at the same time to say that the parts of the Universe are constituted so as to change, and also to wonder

and fret at change or dissolution, as if it were something against the course of Nature; especially as everything is dissolved into the elements out of which it arose. For there is either a scattering of the elements of which a thing was constructed, or a conversion of these, of the solid into earth, of the spiritual into air. So that these constituents are resumed into the system of the Universe, which either undergoes periodical conflagration, or is renewed by never-ending changes. And do not imagine that you had all your earthy and aerial matter from your birth. For the whole of this was an accession of yesterday or the day before, from your food and from the air you breathed. It is this accession which changes, and not what your mother bore. And granting that this recent accession may incline you more to what is individual in your constitution; yet, I think, it alters nothing of what has just been said.

---

8. Having taken to yourself these titles: good, modest, true, prudent, even-tempered, and magnanimous, look to it that you change them not; and, if you should come to lose them, seek them straightway again. And remember that prudence means for you reasoned observation

of all things, and careful attention; even-temper, cheerful acceptance of the lot appointed by universal Nature; magnanimity, the exaltation of the thinking part above any pleasant or painful commotions of the flesh, above vainglory, above death and all such things. If you steadfastly maintain yourself in these titles, with no hankering after hearing them given to you by others, you will be a new man, and a new life will open for you. For to continue as you have been till now, in the same life of distraction and defilement, would mark you as a man devoid of sense, who clings to life like the half-eaten beast fighters, who, though covered with wounds and gore, do yet appeal to be reserved until tomorrow, to be cast again in their wretchedness to the claws and fangs that lacerated them before. Take your stand then on these few titles; and if you are able to abide in them, abide, as one removed to the Islands of the Blessed. But if you perceive that you are falling away, and cannot prevail; have the courage to retire into some corner where you may hope to prevail, or else depart from life altogether, not in anger but in all simplicity, freedom, and modesty, having done at least one thing in life well, by so leaving it. Now it will greatly help you to be mindful of your titles, if you recollect that the Gods desire not adulation, but that reasoning beings should grow in likeness to themselves; and further that a fig tree is set to bear figs, a dog to hunt, a bee to gather honey, and a man to do a man's work.

---

9. Mimes, war, panic, sloth, servility, will wipe out the sacred maxims which you have gathered by observing Nature and stored in your mind. You ought to look and act in every case so that not only shall the task before you be accomplished, but also your theoretic faculty exercised, and the self-confidence which springs from special knowledge preserved without ostentation or affected concealment. Will you ever attain to simplicity; to dignity; to a perfect discrimination in every case as to what a thing really is, what its true place in the Universe, what the time it may endure, what its composition, to whom it may belong, and who can give and take it away?

---

10. The spider exults when he has captured a fly; one man because he has taken a little hare, another because he has netted an anchovy, another because he has hunted down a wild boar or a bear; and another because he has conquered the Sarmatians. But are they not brigands all, if you look to their principles.

11. Acquire a method of perceiving how all things change into one another. Pursue this branch of Philosophy and continually exercise yourself therein. There is nothing so proper as this for cultivating greatness of mind. He who does so has already put off the body; and, having realized how soon he must depart from among men and leave all earthly things behind him, he resigns himself entirely to justice in all his own actions, and to the law of the Universe in everything else which happens. As for what any one may say or think of him or do against him, he gives it not a thought, but contents himself with these two things: to do justly what he has in hand, and to love the lot appointed for him. Such a man has thrown off all hurry and bustle; and has no other will but this, to keep the straight path according to the law, and to follow God whose path is ever straight.

---

12. What need for suspicion when it is open for you to consider what ought to be done? If you see your way, proceed in it calmly, inflexibly. If you do not see it, pause and consult the best advisers. If any other obstacle arise, proceed with prudent caution, according to the means

you have; keeping always close to what appears just. That is the best to which you can attain: and failure in that is the only proper miscarriage. He who in everything follows reason is always at leisure, yet ever ready for action, always cheerful, yet composed.

---

13. As soon as you awake ask yourself: Will it be of consequence to you if what is just and good be done by some other man? It will not. Have you forgotten what manner of men in bed and at table are those who make such display in praise and blame of others; what they do, what they shun and what they pursue; how they steal and how they rob, not with hands and feet but with their most precious part, whereby, if a man will, he may gain faith, modesty, truth, law, a good directing spirit?

---

14. To Nature, which gives and again resumes all things, the well-instructed, modest man will say: "Give what you will; take again what you will." And this he says, not with ostentation, but out of pure obedience and good will to Nature.

15. What remains to you of this life is little. Live as on a mountain. For it makes no difference whether we live here or there, provided we live like citizens everywhere in the world. Let men see and know you as a man indeed, living according to Nature. If they cannot endure you, let them slay you. It is better so than to live as they live.

16. Discourse no more of what a good man should be; but be one.

17. Constantly imagine all time and all existence; and think that every individual thing is in substance a fig seed, and in time the turn of an auger.

18. Consider each of the things around you as already dissolving, in a state of change, and as it were corrupting and being dissipated, or as, one and all, formed by Nature to die.

19. What sort of men are they when they are eating, sleeping, procreating, easing nature, and the like? Then see them lording it over their fellows, puffed up with pride, angry, or issuing judgments from on high! To how many were they slaves but lately, and why? And in what case will they shortly be?

---

20. That is for the advantage of every man which is brought by universal Nature; and for his advantage at the very time at which she brings it.

---

21. "Earth loves the rain;" "and the majestic Ether loves." The Universe loves to bring about whatever is coming to be. I then will say to the Universe: "What you love I love." Is it not a common saying that, "so-and-so loves to happen?"

---

22. Either you are living here your accustomed life; or you are going abroad, and that at your own will: or you are dying, and your public office is discharged. Now, besides these there is nothing. Be therefore of good courage.

23. Keep this ever clear before you: that a country retreat is just like any other place. All things here go the same as on a mountain top, or on the sea beach, or where you will. You may always find that life of the wise man who, in Platonic phrase, "makes the city wall serve him for a shepherd's fold on the mountains."

24. What is my soul to me? What am I making of it, and to what purpose am I now using it? Is it void of understanding? Is it loosened and rent from the great community? Is it glued to, and mingled with, the flesh so as to follow each fleshly motion?

25. Whoever flies from his master is a runaway. Our master is the law, and the law-breaker is a runaway; and so is he also who through grief, or anger, or fear will not acquiesce in something that has happened, is happening, or will happen, in the course of things predestined by the all-ruling power which is the law, laying down for every man what is proper for him. He then who is afraid or grieved or angry, is a runaway.

26. He who has cast seed into the womb departs; another cause takes and works upon it and completes the child. How wonderful the result from such a beginning! The child, again, takes food down its throat; another cause takes and transforms it into sensation, motion, in a word into life and strength and other things, how many and surprising! Consider then these things happening in such hidden ways, and view the power which produces them just as we perceive the gravitation and levitation of bodies; not indeed with our eyes, yet none the less clearly.

---

27. Continually reflect that all that is happening now happened exactly in the same way before; and reflect that the like will happen again. Place before your eyes all that you have ever known from your own experience or from ancient history; dramas and scenes, all similar; such as the whole court of Hadrianus, the whole court of Antoninus, the whole court of Philip, of Alexander, of Croesus. All these were similar, only the actors different.

28. Imagine ever one who is grieved or storms about anything whatever, to be like the pig in a sacrifice, which kicks and screams under the knife. Such, too, is he who, on his couch, deplores in silence, by himself, that we are all tied to our fate. Reflect also that only to a rational being is it given to submit to what happens willingly; the bare submission is a necessity upon all.

---

29. Look attentively on each particular thing you do, and ask yourself if death be a terror because it deprives you of this.

---

30. When you are offended at any one's fault, turn at once to yourself and consider of what similar fault you yourself are guilty; such as esteeming for good things, money, pleasure, a little glory, or the like. By fixing your attention on this you will speedily forget your anger, especially if it occurs to you that he acts under compulsion and cannot do otherwise; else, if it be in your power, relieve him from the compulsion.

31. When you have seen Satyrio the Socratic, think of Eutyches or Hymen; when you have seen Euphrates, think of Eutychio or Silvanus. When Alciphron comes before you, think of Tropaeophorus; and when Xenophon think of Crito or Severus. When you look upon yourself think of any of the Caesars, and with every man likewise. Then let this occur to you: Where, now, are these? Nowhere; or who can tell? For thus you will see all human things to be smoke and nothingness; especially if you call to mind that what has once been changed will never exist again through all the infinity of time. Why then this concern? And why does it not suffice you to live out your short span in well-ordered wise? What material, what a subject for Philosophy you are shunning! For what are all earthly things but exercises for the rational power, when it has viewed all things that occur in life accurately and in their natural order? Abide then until you have assimilated all these things, as a strong stomach assimilates every variety of food, as a bright fire turns whatever you throw upon it into flame and radiance.

32. Let no man have it in his power to say with truth of you that you are not a man of simplicity, candor, and goodness. But let him prove to be mistaken who holds any such opinion of you. This is quite in your power; for who shall hinder you from being good and single-hearted? Only do you determine to live no longer if you cannot be such a man; for neither does reason require, in that case, that you should.

---

33. In the present matter what is the soundest that can be done or said? For, whatever that may be, you are at liberty to do or say it. Make no excuses as if hindered. You will never cease from groaning until your disposition is such that what luxury is to men of pleasure, that to you is doing what is suitable to the constitution of man on every occasion that is thrown or falls in your way. You should regard as enjoyment everything which you are at liberty to do in accordance with your own proper nature; and this liberty you have everywhere. Now to the cylinder it is not given to move everywhere with its proper motion; nor to water, nor to fire, nor to any other thing that is governed by a natural law only, or by a soul irrational; for there are many

circumstances which constrain and stop them. But intelligent reason can pursue through every obstacle the course for which it was created, and which it wills to follow. Set before your eyes this ease with which reason makes its way through all obstacles, as fire goes upwards, a stone downwards, or a cylinder down a slope, and seek for nothing further. The rest of man's difficulties are merely of the body, the lifeless part of him; or else they are such as cannot crush, or in any way injure him save through opinion, or the surrender of reason itself: otherwise, he who suffered by them would himself straightway become evil. In the case of all other organisms, when mishap befalls, the sufferer is thereby rendered worse. But in this respect, it may be said that a man becomes better and more praiseworthy by rightly using his circumstances. In fine, remember that nothing which hurts not the city hurts the man who is by nature a citizen; nor does that hurt the city which hurts not the law. Now, none of the things called misfortunes can hurt the law. Accordingly, what hurts not the law can hurt neither city nor citizen.

34. To the man who is penetrated with true principles, the shortest, the most common hint is a sufficient memorial to keep him free of sorrow and fear. Such as:

Some leaves the winds blow down: the fruitful wood

Breeds more meanwhile, which in springtide appear.

Of men thus ends one race, while one is born.

Your children are leaves; leaves, too, the creatures who confidently cry aloud and deal out eulogy, or, it may be, curses; or who carp and jeer in secret. Leaves, likewise, are they who transmit our fame to posterity. All these "in springtide appear;" then the wind shakes them down, and the forest grows more to take their places. Shortness of life is common to all things, yet you shun and pursue them, as though they were to have no ending. But a little and you will fall asleep; and anon others shall mourn for him who carried your bier.

35. The healthy eye ought to look on everything visible, and not to say, "I want green," like an eye that is diseased. Sound hearing or sense of smell ought to be ready for all that can be heard or smelt; and the healthy stomach should be equally disposed for all sorts of food, as a mill for all that it was built to grind. So also the healthy mind should be ready for all things that happen. That mind which says, "Let my children be spared, and let men applaud my every action," is as an eye which begs for green, or as teeth which require soft food.

---

36. There is no man so happily fated but that when he is dying some bystander will rejoice at the doom which is coming upon him. Were he a virtuous and wise man; will not someone at the last say within himself: "At last I shall breathe freely, unoppressed by this pedagogue. He was not indeed hard on any of us; but I always felt that he tacitly condemned us?" This they would say of a good man. But, in my own case, how many more reasons are there why a multitude would rejoice to be rid of me? You will reflect on this when dying, and depart with the less regret when you consider: "I am leaving a life from which my very partners, for whom I toiled, and

prayed, and planned, are wishing me to begone; hoping, it may be, to gain some additional advantage from my departure." Why then should one strive for a longer sojourn here? Yet let not your parting with them be less pleasant on this account. Preserve your own character, remain to them friendly, benevolent, gracious. On the other hand, depart from your fellow men, not as if torn away; but let your going be like that of one who dies an easy death, whose soul is gently released from the body. Nature knit and cemented you to your fellows, but now she parts you from them. I part, then, as from relations, not reluctant, but unconstrained. For death, too, is a thing accordant with nature.

---

37. Accustom yourself as much as possible, when any one takes any action, to consider only: To what end is he working? But begin at home; and examine yourself first of all.

---

38. Remember that the mover of the puppet strings is the hidden principle within. It is that which is eloquence; that which is life; that, if I may say so, which is the man. Never, in your

imagination, confound that principle with the surrounding earthen vessel and the little organs that are kneaded on to it. Excepting that they grow upon us, they are like the carpenter's axe; since, without the moving and restraining principle, none of these parts in itself is of any greater service than the shuttle to the weaver, the pen to the writer, or the whip to the charioteer.

THE ELEVENTH BOOK

1. These are the characteristics of the rational soul: It beholds itself; it regulates itself in every part; it fashions itself as it wills; the fruit it bears itself enjoys, whereas the products of plants and of the lower animals are enjoyed by others. It reaches its individual end, wheresoever the close of life may overtake it. In a dance or an actor's part any interruption spoils the completeness of the whole action. Not so with the rational soul. At whatever point in its action, or wheresoever it is overtaken by death, it makes its part complete and all-sufficient; so that it can say, "I have received what is mine." Also, it ranges through the whole universe, and the void around it, and discerns its plan. It stretches forth into limitless eternity, and grasps the periodical regeneration of all things, seeing

and comprehending that those who come after us will see nothing new, and that those that went before saw no more than we have seen. Nay, a man of forty, of any tolerable understanding, has, because of the uniformity of things, seen, in a manner, all that has been or will be. Characteristic of the rational soul also are: Love to all around us, truth, modesty; and respect for itself above all other things, which is characteristic also of the general law. Thus, there is no discordance between right reason and the reason of justice.

---

2. You will think little of a pleasing song, a dance, or a gymnastic display, if you analyze the melody into its separate notes, and ask yourself regarding each, "Does this impress me?" You will blush to own it; and so also if you analyze the dance into its single motions and postures, and if you similarly treat the gymnastic display. In general then, except as regards virtue and virtuous action, remember to recur to the constituent parts of things, and by dissecting to despise them; and transfer this practice to life as a whole.

3. How happy is the soul that stands ready to part from the body when it must, and either to be extinguished or to be scattered, or to survive! But let this readiness arise from individual judgment, not from mere obstinacy, as with the Christians, but deliberately, with dignity, and with no affected air of tragedy; so that others may be led to a like disposition.

---

4. Have I done anything for the common good? Is not this itself my advantage? Let this thought be ever with you, and desist not.

---

5. What is your art? Well doing. And how else can this come than from sound general principles regarding Nature as a whole, and the constitution of man in particular?

---

6. First of all, tragedy was introduced to remind us that certain events happen, and are fated to happen as they do; and to teach us that what entertains us on the stage should not grieve us

on the greater stage of the world. You see that such things must be accomplished; and that even they bore them who cried aloud, O Cithaeron! Our dramatic poets have said some excellent things; especially the following:

Me and my children, if the Gods neglect,
It is for some good reason—

and again,

Vain is all anger at external things;

and,

To reap our life like ears of ripened corn—

and the like.

And after tragedy came the Old Comedy, using a schoolmaster's freedom of speech, and employing plain language with great profit to inculcate the duty of humility. To this end Diogenes used a method much the same. Next consider the nature of the Middle Comedy; and lastly for what purpose the New was introduced, which gradually degenerated into the mere ingenuity of artificial mimicry. It is well known that some useful things were said by the New Comic Writers; but what useful end had they in view in all their accumulated poetry and playmaking?

---

7. How manifest it is that no other course of life was more adapted to the practice of philosophy than that which now is yours.

---

8. A branch cut off from its adjacent branch must necessarily be severed from the whole tree. Even so a man, parted from any fellow man, has fallen away from the whole social community. Now a branch is cut off by some external agency; but a man by his own action separates himself from his neighbor—by hatred and aversion, unaware that he has thus torn himself away from the universal polity. Yet there is always given us the good gift of Zeus, who founded the great community, whereby it is in our power to be reingrafted on our kind, and to become once more, natural parts completing the whole. Yet the frequent happening of such separations, makes the reunion and restoration of the separated member more and more difficult. And in general, a branch which has grown from the

first upon a tree, and remained a living part of it, is not like one which has been cut and reingrafted; as the gardeners would say, they are of the same growth but of different persuasion.

---

9. As those who oppose you in the path of right reason have no power to divert you from sane action, so let them not turn you away from amenity towards themselves. Be watchful alike to persist in stable judgment and action, and in meekness towards those who would hinder or otherwise molest you. It is equally weak to grow angry with them or to desist from action and submit to defeat. Both are equally deserters— he who runs away, and he who refuses to stand by friend and kinsman.

---

10. Nature cannot be inferior to Art. The Arts are but imitations of Nature. If this be so, that Nature which is the most perfect and comprehensive of all cannot be inferior to the best artistic skill. Now all Arts use inferior material for higher purposes; so also then does universal Nature. Hence the origin of justice, from which again the other virtues spring.

Justice cannot be preserved if we are solicitous about things indifferent, if we are easily deceived, rash, and changeable.

---

11. If those things, the pursuit and avoidance of which trouble you, come not to you; but, as it happens, you go to them; then let your judgment be at peace concerning them, they will remain motionless, and you will no more be seen pursuing or avoiding them.

---

12. The sphere of the soul attains to perfect shape when it neither expands to what is without, nor contracts upon what is within; neither wrinkles nor collapses, but shines with a radiance whereby it discerns the truth of all things, both without itself and within.

---

13. Does any man contemn me? Let him look to that. And let me look to it that I be found doing or saying nothing worthy of his contempt. Does anyone hate me? That is his affair. I shall be kind and good-natured to everyone, and ready

to shew his mistake to him that hates me; not in order to upbraid him, or to make a show of my patience, but from genuine goodness, like Phocion, if he indeed was sincere. Your inward character should be such that the Gods may see you neither angry nor repining at anything. What evil is it for you now to act according to your nature, and to accept now what is seasonable to the nature of the Universe; you, a man appointed to do some service for the common good?

14. Although they despise, yet they flatter one another. Although they desire to overtop, yet they cringe to one another.

15. How rotten and insincere is his profession who says, "I mean to deal straightforwardly with you." What are you doing, man? There is no need for such a preface. It will appear of itself. Such a profession should be written clearly on your forehead. A man's character should shine forth clearly from his eyes; as the beloved sees that he is so in the glances of those that love him. The straightforward, good man should be like one of

rank odor who can be recognized by the passer by as soon as he approaches, whether he will or no. The ostentation of straightforwardness is the knife under the cloak. Nothing is baser than wolf-friendship. Shun it above all things. The good, straightforward, kindly man bears all these qualities in his eyes, and is not to be mistaken.

---

16. To live the best life is within the power of the soul, if it be indifferent to indifferent things. And it will be indifferent if it looks on all such things, severally and wholly, with discrimination; mindful that not one of them can impose upon us an opinion concerning itself, or can come of itself to us. Things stand motionless without; and it is we that form opinions about them within, and, as it were, write these opinions upon our hearts. We may avoid so writing them; or, if one has crept in unawares, we may instantly blot it out. 'Tis but for a short time that we shall need this vigilance, and then life will cease. For the rest, why should we hold this to be difficult? If it be according to Nature, rejoice in it, and it will become easy for you. If it be contrary to Nature, search out what suits your nature, and follow it diligently, even though it be attended with no glory; for every man will be forgiven for seeking his own proper good.

17. Consider whence each thing came, of what it was compounded, into what it will be changed, how it will be with it when changed, and that it will suffer no evil.

---

18. As to those who offend me, let me consider: First, how I am related to mankind; that we are formed, the one for the other; and that, in another respect, I was set over them as the ram over the flock, and the bull over the herd. Consider yet more deeply, thus: There is either an empire of atoms, or an intelligent Nature governing the whole. If the latter, the inferior beings are created for the superior, and the superior for each other.

Secondly: Consider what manner of men they are at table, in bed, or elsewhere; and especially by what principles they hold themselves bound, and with what arrogance they entertain them.

Thirdly: If they act rightly, we ought not to take it amiss; and, if not rightly, manifestly they do so without intention and in ignorance. For no soul is willingly deprived of truth, or of the faculty of treating every man as he deserves. Accordingly, men are grieved to be called unjust, ungrateful, greedy, and, in short, sinners against their neighbors.

Fourthly: You yourself do often sin, and are no better than another. And, if you abstain from certain sins, still you have the disposition to commit them, even if through cowardice, fear for your character, or other meanness, you hold back.

Fifthly: You cannot even be perfectly sure that wrong has been done, for many things admit of justification. And, generally speaking, a man must have learned much before he can pronounce surely upon the conduct of others.

Sixthly: When you are vexed or worried overmuch, remember that man's life is but for a moment, and that in a little we shall all be laid to rest.

Seventhly: It is not the acts of others that disturb us. Their actions reside in their own souls. Our own opinions alone disturb us. Away with them then; will that you entertain no thought of calamity befallen you, and the anger is gone. But how remove them? By reasoning that there is no dishonor; for, if you hold not that dishonor alone is evil, verily you must fall into many crimes, you may become a robber, or any sort of villain.

Eighthly: How much worse evils we suffer from anger and grief about certain things than from the things themselves about which these passions arise.

Ninthly: Meekness is invincible if it be genuine, without simper or hypocrisy. For what can the most insolent of men do to you, if you persist in civility towards him; and, if occasion offers, admonish him gently and deliberately, shew him the better way at the very moment that he is endeavoring to harm you? "Nay, my son; we were born for something better. No hurt can come to me; it is yourself you hurt, my son." And point out to him delicately, and as a general principle, how the matter stands; that bees and other gregarious animals do not act like him. But this must be done without irony or reproach, rather with loving-kindness and no bitterness of spirit; not as though you were reading him a lesson, or seeking admiration from any bystander, but as if you designed your remarks for him alone, though others may be present.

Remember these nine precepts as gifts received from the Muses; and begin now to be human for the rest of your life. Beware equally of being angry with men and of flattering them.

Both are unsocial and lead to mischief. In all anger recollect that wrath is not becoming to a man; but that meekness and gentleness, as they are more human, are also more manly. Strength and nerves and courage are the portion of the meek and gentle man; and not of the irascible and impatient. For the nearer a man attains to freedom from passion, the nearer he comes to strength. A weak man in grief is like a weak man in anger. Both are hurt, and both give way.

If you want a tenth gift, from the Leader of the Muses, take this: To expect the wicked not to sin is madness. It is to expect an impossibility. But to allow them to injure others, and to forbid them to injure you, is foolish and tyrannical.

---

19. There are four states of the soul against which you must continually and especially be upon your guard; and which, when detected, should be effaced, by remarking thus of each. "This thought is unnecessary. This tends to social dissolution. You could not say this from your heart; and to speak otherwise than from the heart you must regard as the most absurd conduct." And, fourthly, whatever causes self-reproach is

an overpowering or subjection of the diviner part within you to the less honorable and mortal part, the body, and to its grosser tendencies.

---

20. The serial and igneous parts of which you are compounded, although they naturally tend upwards, nevertheless obey the general law of the Universe, and are retained here in composition. The earthy and humid parts of you, though they naturally tend downwards, are nevertheless supported and remain where they are, although not in their natural situation. Thus, the elements, wheresoever placed by the superior power, obey the whole; waiting till the signal shall sound again for their dissolution. Is it not grievous that the intellectual part alone should be disobedient, and fret at its function? Yet is no violence done to it, nothing imposed contrary to its nature. Still, it is impatient, and tends to opposition. For all its tendencies towards injustice, debauchery, wrath, sorrows, and fears are so many departures from Nature. And, when the soul frets at any particular event, it is deserting its appointed station. It is formed for holiness and piety toward God, no less than for justice. These last are branches of social goodness even more venerable than the practice of justice.

21. He whose aim in life is not always one and the same cannot himself be one and the same through his whole life. But singleness of aim is not sufficient, unless you consider also what that aim ought to be. For, as there is not agreement of opinion regarding all those things which are reckoned good by the majority, but only as regards some of them such as are of public utility; so, your aim should be social and political. For he alone who directs all his personal aims to such an end can reach a uniform course of conduct, and thus be ever the same man.

---

22. Remember the country mouse and the town mouse; and how the latter feared and trembled.

---

23. Socrates called the maxims of the vulgar hobgoblins, bogies to frighten children.

---

24. The Spartans at their public shows set seats for strangers in the shade, but sat themselves where they found room.

25. Socrates made this excuse for not going to Perdiccas upon his invitation: "Lest I should come to the worst of all ends, by receiving favors which I could not return."

26. In the writings of the Ephesians there is a precept, frequently to call to remembrance some of those who cultivated virtue of old.

27. The Pythagoreans recommended that we should look at the heavens in the morning, to put us in mind of beings that go on doing their proper work uniformly and continuously; and of their order, purity and naked simplicity; for there is no veil upon a star.

28. Think of Socrates clad in a skin, when Xanthippe had taken his cloak and gone out; and what he said to his friends, who were ashamed, and would have left him when they saw him dressed in such an extraordinary fashion.

29. In writing and reading you must be led before you can lead. Much more is this so in life.

---

30. *Yourself a slave, your speech cannot be free.*

---

31. *And my heart laughed within me.*

---

32. *Virtue herself they blame with harshest words.*

---

33. To look for figs in winter is madness; and so, it is to long for a child that may no longer be yours.

---

34. Epictetus said that, when you kiss your child, you should whisper within yourself: "Tomorrow perhaps he may die." "Ill-omened words!" say you. "The words have no evil omen," says he, "but simply indicate an act of Nature. Is it of evil omen to say the corn is reaped?"

35. The green grape, the ripe cluster, the dried grape are all changes, not into nothing, but into that which is not at present.

---

36. No man can rob you of your liberty of action; as has been said by Epictetus.

---

37. He tells us also that we must find out the true art of assenting; and in treating of our impulses, he says that we must be vigilant in restraining them, that they may act with proper reservation, with public spirit, with due sense of proportion; also, that we should refrain utterly from sensual passion; and not be restive in matters where we have no control.

---

38. The contention is not about any chance matter, said he, but as to whether we are insane or sane

39. "What do you desire?" says Socrates. "To have the souls of rational beings or of irrational? Rational. Rational of what kind, virtuous or vicious? Virtuous. Why then do you not seek after such souls? Because we have them already. Why then do you fight and stand at variance?"

THE TWELFTH BOOK

1. All that you desire to compass by devious means is yours already, if you will but freely take it. That is to say, if you will leave behind you all that is past, commit the future to Providence, and regulate the present in piety and justice. In piety that you may love your appointed lot; for Nature gave it to you and you to it. In justice, that you may speak the truth without constraint or guile; that you may do what is lawful and proper; that you may not be hindered by the wickedness of others, or by their opinion, or their talk, or by any sensation of this poor surrounding body, for the part concerned may look to that. If then, now that you are near your exit, setting behind you all other things, you will hold alone in reverence your ruling part, the spirit divine within you; if you will cease to dread the end of life, but rather

fear to miss the beginning of life according to Nature, you will be a man, worthy of the ordered Universe that produced you; you will cease to be a stranger in your own country, gaping in wonder at every daily happening, caught up by this trifle or by that.

God beholds all souls bare and stripped of these corporeal vessels, husk, and refuse. By his intelligence alone he touches that only which has been instilled by him and has emanated from himself. If you would but inure yourself to do the like, you would be eased of many a torment. For he who regards not the surrounding flesh will not waste his leisure in thinking about vesture, house, or fame, or other mere external furniture or accoutrement.

Three parts there are of which you are compact; body, soul, intelligence. Of these the two first are yours in so far as they must have your care; the third only is properly your own. And if you will cast away from yourself, that is from your mind, all that others do or say, all that you yourself have done or said, all your fears for the future, all the uncontrollable accompaniments of the body that envelops you and of its congenital soul, and all that is whirled in the besieging vortex that races without, so that your intellectual power, made pure, and set above the accidents of fate, may live its own life in freedom, just, resigned, veracious; if, I repeat, you cast out from your soul all comes of excessive attachment either to the past or to the future, then you will become in the words of Empedocles:

A faultless sphere rejoiced in endless rest.

You will study to live the only life there is to live, to wit the present; and you will be able, till death shall come, to spend what remains of life in noble tranquility, at peace with the spirit within.

---

4. I have wondered often how it comes that, while every man loves himself beyond all others, yet he holds his own opinion of himself in less esteem than the opinion of others. Yet, if a God or some wise teacher came and ordered a man to conceive and design nothing which he would not utter the moment it occurred to him, he would not abide the ordeal for a single day. Thus, we stand in greater awe of our neighbors' opinion of us than we do of our own.

5. How can it be that the Gods, who have ordered all things well for man's advantage, overlooked one thing only, to wit that some of the best of mankind, who have held the closest relations with things divine, and by pious works and holy ministry become intimate with the Divinity, once dead, should arise no more, but be altogether extinguished? If this be truly so, be well assured that, if it ought to have been otherwise, they would have made it otherwise. Had it been right it would have been practicable; and had it been according to Nature, Nature would have effected it. From its not being so, if it really be not so, be persuaded that it ought not to have been. You see that, in debating this matter, you are pleading a point of justice with the Gods. Now we would not thus plead with the Gods were they not perfectly good and just. And, if they are so, they have left nothing unjustly and unreasonably neglected in their administration.

---

6. Essay even tasks that you despair of executing. The left hand, which in other things is of little value for want of use, yet holds the bridle more firmly than the right, for in this it has practice.

7. Consider how death ought to find you, both as to body and as to soul. Think of the shortness of life, of the eternities before and after, and of the infirmity of all material things.

---

8. Contemplate the fundamental causes stripped of disguises. Think what pain is, what pleasure is, what death, and what fame. Consider how many are themselves the causes of all the disquiet that they suffer; how no man may be hindered by another; how all is matter of opinion.

---

9. In the use of principles, we should be like the pugilist rather than the swordsman. For when the latter drops the sword which he uses he is undone. But the former has his hand always by him and needs but to wield it.

---

10. Consider well the nature of things, distinguishing between matter, cause, and purpose.

11. What a glorious power is given to man, never to do any action of which God will not approve, and to welcome whatever God appoints for him!

12. As to what happens in the course of nature, the Gods are not to be blamed. They never do wrong, willingly or unwillingly. Neither are men to be blamed, for they do no wrong willingly. There is therefore none to blame.

13. How ridiculous, and how like a foreigner, is he who is surprised at anything which happens in life!

14. There is either a fatal necessity, an unalterable order, or a placable Providence, or a blind confusion without a governor. If there be an unalterable necessity, why strive against it? If there be a Providence admitting of propitiation, make yourself worthy of the divine aid. If there be an ungoverned confusion, be comforted; seeing that in this tempest you have within yourself a guiding intelligence. And, if the wave

should carry you away, let it carry away the carcass and the animal life, for the intellectual part of you it will not carry away.

---

15. If the light of a lamp shine and lose not its radiance until it be extinguished, shall truth, justice, and temperance be extinguished in you before your own extinction.

---

16. When you have the impression that a man has sinned, say to yourself: "How do I know that this is sin?" And, if he has sinned, consider that he stands self-condemned: and thus, as it were, has torn his own face.

He that would wish the wicked not to sin is like one who would have the fig tree not have juice in its figs, would have infants not cry, horses not neigh, and other inevitable things not happen. What shall the wicked man do, having a wicked disposition? If you are so keen, cure it.

---

17. If a thing be not becoming, do it not; if not true, say it not.

18. Endeavor always to see in everything what it is that causes your impression; and unfold it by distinguishing the cause, the matter, the relation to other things, and the period within which it must cease to exist.

---

19. Perceive at last that there is within you something better and more divine than the immediate cause of your sensations of pleasure and pain; something, in short, beyond the strings which move the puppet. What is now my thought? Is it fear? Suspicion? Lust? Or any such passion?

---

20. In the first place, let nothing be done at random or without an object. In the second let your object never be other than the common good.

---

21. Yet a little, and you shall be no more; nor shall any of these things remain which you now behold, nor any of those who are now living. It is the nature of all things to change, to turn, and to corrupt; in order that other things may, in

22. Reflect that everything is matter of opinion; and opinion rests with yourself, suppress then your opinion, what time you will, and like one who has doubled the cape and reached the bay, you will have calm and stillness everywhere, never a wave.

---

23. Any one natural operation, ending at its proper time, suffers no ill by ceasing, nor does the agent therein suffer any ill by its thus ceasing. In like manner, as to the whole series of actions which is life, if it ends in its season, it suffers no ill by ceasing, nor is he who thus completes his series, in any evil case. The season and the term are assigned by Nature; sometimes even by your own nature, as in old age; but always by the nature of the whole, by the interchange of whose parts the Universe still remains fresh and in its bloom. Now, that is always good and seasonable which is advantageous to the nature of the whole. Wherefore the ceasing of life cannot be evil to the individual. There is no turpitude in it, since it is beyond our power, and contains nothing contrary to the common advantage. Nay, it is good, since it is seasonable and advantageous to the whole, and, congruent with the order of the Universe. Thus, too, he is led by God who goes the same way with God, and that by like inclination.

24. Have these three thoughts always at hand: First, as to your action, do nothing inconsiderately, or otherwise than justice herself would have acted. As for external events, they either happen by chance or by providence; now, no man should quarrel with chance or censure providence. Second, examine what each thing is, from its seed to its quickening; and from its quickening to its death; of what materials it is composed, and into what it will be resolved. Third, reflect that could you be raised on high, and from thence behold all human affairs, you would discern their great variety, conscious at the same time of the crowds of serial and ethereal inhabitants around us; but were you so raised ever so often, you would always see the same things, all uniform and of brief duration. Can we set our pride on such matters?

---

25. "Cast away opinion, and you are saved." Who then hinders you from casting it away?

---

26. When you fret at anything, you have forgotten that all happens in accordance with the nature of the Universe, and that the wrong done was

another's. This, too, that whatever happens has happened, and will happen, and is now happening everywhere. You have also forgotten how great is the bond between any man and all the human race, a bond not of blood and seed, but of common intelligence. You have forgotten that the intelligence of every man is divine, and an efflux from God; also, that no man is proprietor of anything: his children, his body, his very life are given of God. You have forgotten, too, that everything is matter of opinion; and that it is the present moment only that one can live or lose.

---

27. Bring to frequent recollection those who have grieved about anything overmuch, those who have been pre-eminent in the extreme of glory or misfortune, in feuds or other circumstances of fate. Then stop and ask, "Where are they all now?" Smoke and ashes, and an old tale; or perhaps not even a tale. Pass them all in review: Fabius Catullinus in the country, Lucius Lupus in his gardens, Stertinius at Baiae, Tiberius at Capreae, Velius Rufus, and, in fine, all eminence attended with the high regard of men. How cheap is all that is so eagerly pursued? And how much better does it become a

philosopher to show himself, in the part of the material world allotted to him, just, temperate, and obedient to the Gods; and this with simplicity; for most intolerable of all is the pride of false humility.

---

28. To those who ask, "Where have you seen the Gods, and how assured yourself of their existence, that you worship them?" make this reply: First, they are visible, even to the eye. Again, my own soul I cannot see, and yet I reverence it. Thus, too, as regards the Gods, I continually feel their power; and so, I know that they exist, and I worship them.

---

29. The safety of life is to see the whole nature of everything, and to discern the matter and the form of its constitution; also, to do justice with all your heart, and to speak the truth. What remains but to enjoy life, adding one good to an another, so as not to lose the smallest interval?

30. There is but one light of the sun, although it be scattered upon walls and hills, and a myriad other objects. There is but one common substance, although it be divided among ten thousand bodies having as many different qualities. There is but one soul, though it be distributed among countless different natures and individual forms. There is but one intelligent spirit, though it may seem to be divided. The other parts of these individuals of which we have spoken, such as breath and matter, are void of perception and of mutual affection; yet even they are held together by the intelligent spirit and gravitate together. But intelligence has a special tendency to its kind, and unites therewith, and the community of feeling is not broken.

---

31. What do you desire? To live on? Or is it to feel or to desire? To grow and to decay again? To speak or think? Which of all these seems worthy to be desired? And, if each and all of them is despicable, proceed to the last that remains, to follow reason and God. Now, it is repugnant to reverence for reason and for God to grieve at the loss by death of these other despicable things.

32. How small a part of the boundless immensity of the ages is allotted to each of us, and presently that will vanish in eternity! How little is ours of the universal substance; how little of the universal spirit! On what a little clod of the whole earth do we creep! Considering all this, reckon nothing great except to act as your nature leads you, and to endure what universal Nature brings to pass.

---

33. How is it with your ruling part? On this all depends. All other things, within or without our control, are but corpses, dust, and smoke.

---

34. This most of all must rouse you to despise death: That even those who held pleasure to be good and pain to be evil nevertheless despised it.

---

35. To him who holds that alone to be good which comes in proper season, who cares not whether he has acted oftener or less often according to right reason; to whom it makes no difference

whether he behold the universe for a longer time or a shorter—for this man death also has no terror.

---

36. You have lived, O man, as a citizen of this great city; of what consequence to you whether for five years or for three? What comes by law is fair to all. Where then is the calamity, if you are sent out of the city, by no tyrant or unjust judge, but Nature herself who at first introduced you, just as the praetor who engaged the actor again dismisses him from the stage? "But," say you, "I have not spoken my five acts, but only three." True, but in life three acts make up the play. For he sets the end who was responsible for its composition at the first, and for its present dissolution. You are responsible for neither. Depart then graciously; for he who dismisses you is gracious.